DATE DUE

#47-0108 Peel Off Pressure Sensitive

TRYPANOSOMIASIS

Antibiotic-Resistant Bacteria

Anthrax

Avian Flu

Botulism

Campylobacteriosis

Cervical Cancer

Cholera

Ebola

Encephalitis

Escherichia coli Infections

Gonorrhea

Hantavirus Pulmonary Syndrome

Helicobacter pylori

Hepatitis

Herpes

HIV/AIDS

Infectious Fungi

Influenza

Legionnaire's Disease

Leprosy

Lung Cancer

Lyme Disease

Mad Cow Disease (Bovine Spongiform Encephalopathy)

Malaria

Meningitis

Mononucleosis

Pelvic Inflammatory Disease

Plague

Polio

Prostate Cancer

Rabies

Salmonella

SARS

Smallpox

Streptococcus (Group A)

Syphilis

Toxic Shock Syndrome

Trypanosomiasis

Tuberculosis

Tularemia

Typhoid Fever

West Nile Virus

DEADLY DISEASES AND EPIDEMICS

TRYPANOSOMIASIS

Donald Kruel

FOUNDING EDITOR
The Late I. **Edward Alcamo**
Distinguished Teaching Professor of Microbiology,
SUNY Farmingdale

FOREWORD BY
David Heymann
World Health Organization

CHELSEA HOUSE
PUBLISHERS
An imprint of Infobase Publishing

Dedicated to Ed Alcamo

Deadly Diseases and Epidemics: Trypanosomiasis

Copyright © 2007 by Infobase Publishing

All rights reserved. No part of this book may be reproduced or utilized in any form or by any means, electronic or mechanical, including photocopying, recording, or by any information storage or retrieval systems, without permission in writing from the publisher. For information contact:

Chelsea House
An imprint of Infobase Publishing
132 West 31st Street
New York, NY 10001

ISBN-10: 0-7910-9245-3
ISBN-13: 978-0-7910-9245-3

Library of Congress Cataloging-in-Publication Data
Kruel, Donald.
  Trypanosomiasis / Donald Kruel ; consulting editor I. Edward Alcamo;
foreword by David Heymann.
     p. cm.—(Deadly diseases and epidemics)
  Includes bibliographical references and index.
  ISBN 0-7910-9245-3 (hc : alk. paper)
  1. Trypanosomiasis—Juvenile literature. I. Title. II. Series.
  RC186.T82K78 2006
  616.9'363—dc22   2006012587

Chelsea House books are available at special discounts when purchased in bulk quantities for businesses, associations, institutions, or sales promotions. Please call our Special Sales Department in New York at (212) 967-8800 or (800) 322-8755.

You can find Chelsea House on the World Wide Web at http://www.chelseahouse.com

Series design by Terry Mallon
Cover design by Keith Trego
Illustrations by Richard Garratt
Printed in the United States of America
Bang EJB 10 9 8 7 6 5 4 3 2 1

This book is printed on acid-free paper.

All links and Web addresses were checked and verified to be correct at the time of publication. Because of the dynamic nature of the Web, some addresses and links may have changed since publication and may no longer be valid.

Table of Contents

In the 1960s, many of the infectious diseases that had terrorized generations were tamed. After a century of advances, the leading killers of Americans both young and old were being prevented with new vaccines or cured with new medicines. The risk of death from pneumonia, tuberculosis (TB), meningitis, influenza, whooping cough, and diphtheria declined dramatically. New vaccines lifted the fear that summer would bring polio, and a global campaign was on the verge of eradicating smallpox worldwide. New pesticides like DDT cleared mosquitoes from homes and fields, thus reducing the incidence of malaria, which was present in the southern United States and which remains a leading killer of children worldwide. New technologies produced safe drinking water and removed the risk of cholera and other water-borne diseases. Science seemed unstoppable. Disease seemed destined to all but disappear.

But the euphoria of the 1960s has evaporated.

The microbes fought back. Those causing diseases like TB and malaria evolved resistance to cheap and effective drugs. The mosquito developed the ability to defuse pesticides. New diseases emerged, including AIDS, Legionnaires', and Lyme disease. And diseases which had not been seen in decades reemerged, as the hantavirus did in the Navajo Nation in 1993. Technology itself actually created new health risks. The global transportation network, for example, meant that diseases like West Nile virus could spread beyond isolated regions and quickly become global threats. Even modern public health protections sometimes failed, as they did in 1993 in Milwaukee, Wisconsin, resulting in 400,000 cases of the digestive system illness cryptosporidiosis. And, more recently, the threat from smallpox, a disease believed to be completely eradicated, has returned along with other potential bioterrorism weapons such as anthrax.

The lesson is that the fight against infectious diseases will never end.

In our constant struggle against disease, we as individuals have a weapon that does not require vaccines or drugs, and that is the warehouse of knowledge. We learn from the history of science that "modern" beliefs can be wrong. In this series of books, for example, you will learn that diseases like syphilis were once thought to be caused by eating potatoes. The invention of the microscope set science on the right path. There are more positive lessons from history. For example, smallpox was eliminated by vaccinating everyone who had come in contact with an infected person. This "ring" approach to smallpox control is still the preferred method for confronting an outbreak, should the disease be intentionally reintroduced.

At the same time, we are constantly adding new drugs, new vaccines, and new information to the warehouse. Recently, the entire human genome was decoded. So too was the genome of the parasite that causes malaria. Perhaps by looking at the microbe and the victim through the lens of genetics we will be able to discover new ways to fight malaria, which remains the leading killer of children in many countries.

Because of advances in our understanding of such diseases as AIDS, entire new classes of antiretroviral drugs have been developed. But resistance to all these drugs has already been detected, so we know that AIDS drug development must continue.

Education, experimentation, and the discoveries that grow out of them are the best tools to protect health. Opening this book may put you on the path of discovery. I hope so, because new vaccines, new antibiotics, new technologies, and, most importantly, new scientists are needed now more than ever if we are to remain on the winning side of this struggle against microbes.

David Heymann
Executive Director
Communicable Diseases Section
World Health Organization
Geneva, Switzerland

1

Parasites: A World Health Problem

While on safari in Tanzania, Africa, an American tourist gazed across the broad savannah. He saw gazelles, wildebeests, zebras, and giraffes through the shimmering heat. It was a peaceful scene, although predators lurked about. A small tsetse fly, one of many regional insect pests, landed on the tourist's bare leg and bit him, taking a drop of blood. The bite stung a little, but that was not the only problem. As it fed, the fly had injected something dangerous. After a few days a painful **chancre** formed. Next came fever, headache, enlarged lymph nodes, and a rash. Without treatment the tourist's brain would eventually become affected, causing sleepiness, coma, and death.

On the continent of South America, about 3,000 miles (4,828 km) to the west, a young girl slept in a small thatched hut in a rain forest. Outside thousands of insects were chirping. Most of the insects were outdoors, but some were in the hut along with the child. A large insect crept from a crevice in the wall toward the sleeping girl. Once on her face, the insect took a blood meal, defecated (eliminated waste from the hindgut) on the wound, and then left. It was a nasty bite, but that was not the worst part of the experience. The kissing bug, while defecating, had placed thousands of live organisms in the girl's wound. A **chagoma**, a type of ulcer, appeared at the wound site first, followed by fever, **malaise**, and enlargement of lymph nodes, spleen, and liver. Without treatment there might have been a deadly progression to the heart and brain.

Figure 1.1 Human trypanosomiasis in its two forms is caused by parasitic organisms that thrive in two very different environments, the savanna in Africa (top) and the rainforest in South America (bottom). WHO/TDR/Baldry (top); © Jacques Jangoux / Photo Researchers, Inc. (bottom)

TRYPANOSOMES CAUSE TRYPANOSOMIASIS

What do these two events have in common? Both humans were infected by a blood parasite called a **trypanosome**, causing a disease called trypanosomiasis. There are African and American types of trypanosomiasis and both are devastating to humans on two continents: Africa and South America. To better understand these diseases, it's best to first examine the way living organisms are classified, and then look at the importance of infectious diseases to the world population.

KINGDOMS OF LIFE AND MICROBES

All around us life exists in wonderful, diverse forms. Plants and animals may be the most evident, but there are other forms of life, including the smallest of these, which are microorganisms, or microbes. Generally invisible to the naked eye, microbes

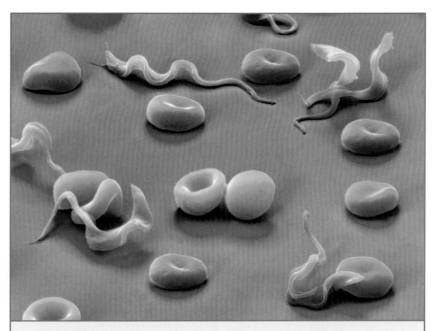

Figure 1.2 Trypanosomes are the blood parasites that cause trypanosomiasis. The twisted, wavy parasites are shown next to the round red blood cells. © Eye of Science / Photo Researchers, Inc.

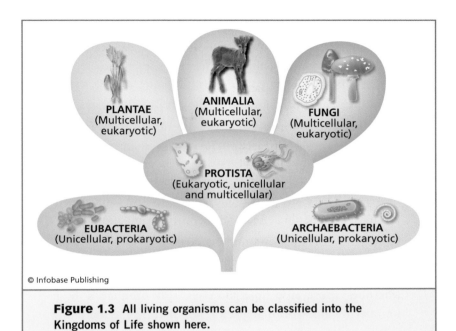

Figure 1.3 All living organisms can be classified into the Kingdoms of Life shown here.

© Infobase Publishing

include viruses, fungi, bacteria, and protists. (Viruses, the smallest infectious organisms, are not placed in a kingdom because they are often not considered living entities and are only able to reproduce inside an infected cell of a living **host** organism. There, they use the cell's own machinery to churn out new virus particles.) The protist group includes algae (plant-like microbes) and protozoa (animal-like microbes). In some systems of classification, slime molds (fungus-like microbes) are also part of the protist group. All together, there are five major Kingdoms of Life and microbes make up three of them. In some newer classifications, there are six kingdoms (Figure 1.3, sidebar page 13).

Microbes are widespread in nature and they even inhabit human beings. It may be difficult to believe, but the total living matter, or **biomass**, of microbes rivals the amount of all the animals and plants on Earth combined. In fact, microorganisms are very important to the health of all living organisms and the functioning of the planet.

Just as there are only a handful of large predatory animals that humans need to fear—such as the grizzly bear, great white shark, and lion—there are relatively few microbes that are harmful to humans, considering how many microbes exist in nature. These dangerous microbes include those responsible for AIDS (HIV virus), tuberculosis (*Mycobacterium tuberculosis*), malaria (*Plasmodium sp.*), influenza (influenza virus), pneumonia (*Streptococcus pneumoniae*), staph infections (*Staphylococcus aureus*), and strep throat (*Streptococcus pyogenes*). These few pathogenic organisms and some others can have catastrophic effects on the world population.

MICROBES CAUSES INFECTIOUS DISEASES WORLDWIDE

Microbes cause infectious diseases and produce a high number of illnesses in a specific population, the **morbidity** rate, which may lead to a high number of deaths, the **mortality** rate, especially in developing nations. Viruses are the culprits in infectious diseases such as influenza, Ebola, and AIDS, while bacteria causes cholera and tuberculosis. Fungi cause fewer diseases and are not as well known, but they are still important. A yeast fungus called *Cryptococcus neoformans*, which is found in soil, can produce a deadly form of meningitis. The filamentous or fuzzy forms of fungi sometimes appear in places such as on old food in the refrigerator. Although each filament is microscopic, a large mass, or **colony**, can be visible to the naked eye. Most fungi of this type break down dead organic matter in nature. However, there are several **systemic** diseases that are caused by specific fungi. *Coccidioides immitis*, for example, is found in the soil of arid areas of the Western Hemisphere. Some filaments or hyphae in the soil break into pieces with thick, barrel shaped cells. These are lightweight and can easily become airborne during windy conditions. Inhalation of such reproductive **arthrospores** can produce an infection that spreads to many organs of the body.

SIX KINGDOMS OF LIFE

Scientists have tried to classify all life-forms into categories to better understand them. This is a difficult task, but to start with, there are basically two types of living organisms based on the smallest unit, the cell. Prokaryotes, which are single-celled bacteria, have relatively simple cells to accomplish their life processes. Eukaryotes, on the other hand, are more complicated and their cells have specialized work areas bounded by membranes. One of these work areas is a defined nucleus, with DNA on chromosomes, and a variety of other organelles for specific tasks. The eukaryotes include animals, plants, fungi, and the protists (protozoa and algae).

With the advent of genetic analysis, scientists found that some prokaryotes were very different from the commonly known species of bacteria called eubacteria (true bacteria). Some felt they belonged in a domain of their own, called archaea (ancient bacteria). Microbes in the archaea group still look generally the same as other bacteria and have prokaryotic cells, but the archaea are found in some very inhospitable environments. These include very salty lakes (much saltier than the ocean) such as the Great Salt Lake in Utah, boiling volcanic pools like those found in Yellowstone National Park, and anaerobic (without oxygen) mud in swamps and under the sea. The archaea are thought to be a very ancient life form that flourished on the early Earth when conditions were different, and they still exist today in a few special habitats. Microbiologists call the archaea *extremophiles* because of their ability to survive and reproduce in places where very few other living organisms could exist.

Some systems of classification still lump the eubacteria and the archaea into one kingdom. Newer classification charts have two kingdoms for the prokaryotes (eubacteria and archaea) plus the other four established kingdoms (protists, fungi, animals, and plants), for a total of six kingdoms.

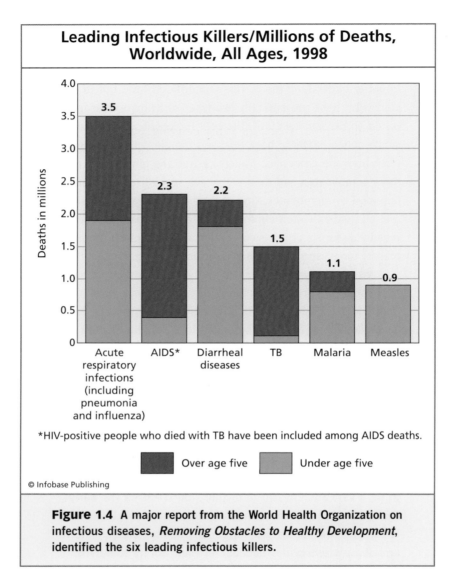

Leading Infectious Killers/Millions of Deaths, Worldwide, All Ages, 1998

*HIV-positive people who died with TB have been included among AIDS deaths.

■ Over age five   ■ Under age five

© Infobase Publishing

Figure 1.4 A major report from the World Health Organization on infectious diseases, *Removing Obstacles to Healthy Development*, identified the six leading infectious killers.

Protozoa, the animal-like microorganisms, also cause diseases. Protozoa cause trypanosomiasis as well as other serious maladies, including malaria. The agents of trypanosomiasis and malaria, which are both transmitted by insects, are considered parasites, along with certain other protozoa, some worms, and a few **arthropods**. Taken all together, the number of parasite infections worldwide compares to, and may surpass, the number of familiar bacterial, fungal, and viral diseases we often hear about.

MAJOR PARASITIC DISEASES

The thought of living organisms entering our bodies and creeping around is repulsive and scary. Science fiction writers know this and have produced many novels and movies based on this theme. Most parasites in movies are aliens from another world, but in fact, there are plenty of parasites to worry about right here on Earth.

The term **parasite** refers to an organism that lives on or inside another organism and derives benefits while it causes harm to the host. Although this definition can apply to all types of pathogenic microbes, we generally use the term *parasite* to refer to infections that are caused by protozoa. A few invertebrates (animals without backbones), such as parasitic worms, are also included in the category of parasites. Microbiologists can often find the microscopic eggs and larvae that parasitic worms leave behind in patients' bodies. In some cases, the adult worm may be found and help doctors provide a diagnosis. Some ticks, fleas, mites, and lice from the arthropod group are called **ectoparasites**. They can live as parasites on the skin of humans and introduce other infectious organisms from their bites and through abrasions of the skin.

Parasitic protozoa and worms take a very heavy toll on the world's population.

PROTOZOA LOCOMOTION

Trypanosomes are part of the protozoa category. Most protozoa are one-celled predators that move around, searching for food. They are, in fact, commonly categorized on the basis of locomotion, or the way they move. The amoeba is a mass of protoplasm that flows by means of **pseudopods** (false feet) to engulf food. Ciliates have tiny hairs, or **cilia**,

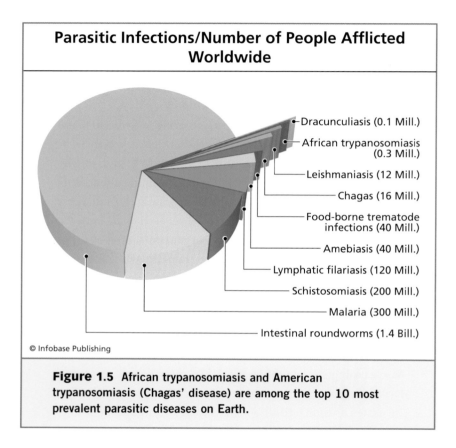

Parasitic Infections/Number of People Afflicted Worldwide

- Dracunculiasis (0.1 Mill.)
- African trypanosomiasis (0.3 Mill.)
- Leishmaniasis (12 Mill.)
- Chagas (16 Mill.)
- Food-borne trematode infections (40 Mill.)
- Amebiasis (40 Mill.)
- Lymphatic filariasis (120 Mill.)
- Schistosomiasis (200 Mill.)
- Malaria (300 Mill.)
- Intestinal roundworms (1.4 Bill.)

© Infobase Publishing

Figure 1.5 African trypanosomiasis and American trypanosomiasis (Chagas' disease) are among the top 10 most prevalent parasitic diseases on Earth.

all over their bodies. With these, they can propel themselves quickly from one food source to another. When a microbiologist or naturalist looks at pond water, these predators seem to be the Olympic swimmers of the microbe group. Flagellates can also move rather quickly by using **flagella** (the singular form is *flagellum*), which are longer, whip-like tails that produce a jerky motion. Some of the members of the protozoa groups mentioned so far are important parasites of man, but most have a free-living existence in nature. That is, they do not harm man or other large animals, but instead prey on other microbes and tiny animals in soil and water. In contrast, the **sporozoa** are all parasites that lack noticeable means of locomotion. Here we have the agent of malaria that lives on the red blood cells of humans. It is one of the most prevalent parasites in the world because of the number of people infected.

THE CAUSE OF TRYPANOSOMIASIS

The protozoan that causes trypanosomiasis is a flagellate and is sometimes called a hemoflagellate, because it swims in the bloodstream along with the red and white blood cells. The agent that causes trypanosomiasis on the American continent is called *Trypanosoma cruzi* (Chagas' disease), and the agents that cause trypanosomiasis on the African continent are two types of *Trypanosoma brucei* named *Trypanosoma brucei gambiense* and *Trypanosoma brucei rhodesiense* (African sleeping sickness). Precise statistics are not available, but it is estimated that *Trypanosoma cruzi* and the human pathogens of *Trypanosoma brucei rhodesiense and Trypanosoma brucei gambiense* affect approximately 15 million in the Americas and 300,000 to 500,000 in Africa. (The names of these protozoa are often abbreviated as *T. cruzi* and *T. brucei.*)

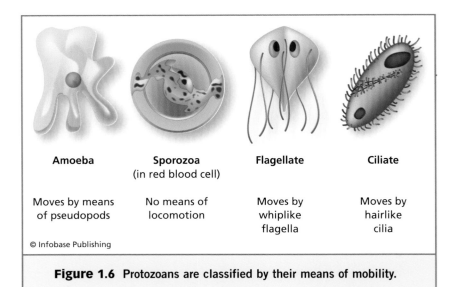

Amoeba	Sporozoa (in red blood cell)	Flagellate	Ciliate
Moves by means of pseudopods	No means of locomotion	Moves by whiplike flagella	Moves by hairlike cilia

© Infobase Publishing

Figure 1.6 Protozoans are classified by their means of mobility.

Some other mammals, birds, fishes, and frogs may also be infected with trypanosomes. The species *T. cruzi, T brucei gambiense,* and *T. brucei rhodesiense,* can be transmitted to humans from some mammals and cause clinical disease but other species cannot. When animal pathogens affect humans, it is called a **zoonosis**. In trypanosomiasis, an insect transmits the trypanosome from an infected animal or another human. The insect is then called a **vector** of the disease.

DISTRIBUTION ON TWO CONTINENTS

It may seem unusual that trypanosomiasis exists in both Africa (the Eastern Hemisphere) and South America (the Western Hemisphere). About 200 million years ago, the continents were not situated the way they are today. All the continents were then part of Pangaea, a "supercontinent" that occupied a large part of the Earth. Over time two huge pieces broke away from Pangaea and started to move away from each other very slowly in a process known as continental drift. At first Pangaea divided into two continents: Laurasia (which included what is now North America, Europe, and Asia) and Gondwanaland (which consisted of present-day Africa, South America, Antarctica, Australia, and India). Approximately 65 to 100 million years ago, Gondwanaland started to break up and the newly formed separate continents slowly moved away with plants, animals, and microbes on each of them. Eventually all living organisms changed. Today the continents of Africa and South America are separated by thousands of miles of ocean. When they were joined as part of Gondwanaland, however, similar trypano-somes existed on both land areas. Over millions of years, these trypanosomes changed, or evolved. It is not clear exactly when *T. cruzi* and *T. brucei* started to diverge, but it appears that there was a great deal of change after the continents separated. There is some molecular evidence that points to this fact.[1] Today *T. cruzi* exists in South America and *T. brucei* exists in Africa. Each has a different vector and disease syndrome with distinct symptoms. Even within Africa, there has been a change in the

Geographic Distribution *Trypanosoma cruzi* (Chagas' disease)	Geographic Distribution of Human African Trypanosomiasis (Sleeping Sickness)
	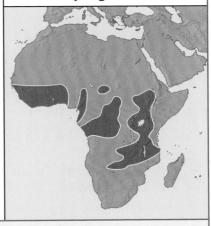

Figure 1.7 Trypanosomes separated on two continents share a common origin from a time millions of years ago when South America and Africa were part of a single large land mass.

structure of *T. brucei*. Although the trypanosomes in East and West Africa look the same, they have drifted apart genetically a bit and they cause slightly different diseases. Therefore, the East African strain is called *Trypanosoma brucei rhodesiense*, while the West African strain is *Trypanosoma brucei gambiense*. The terms *rhodesiense* and *gambiense* are called subspecies of the species name.

2

Overview of African Trypanosomiasis a.k.a. African Sleeping Sickness

In the 19th century the exploration of Africa, primarily by Europeans and traders from the Middle East, was a formidable undertaking. The interior of this huge continent was largely unknown and potentially dangerous. There were ferocious animals, unfamiliar native populations, and rampant diseases. Although there were many courageous explorers, Henry Morton Stanley and David Livingstone are perhaps the best known. In their quest to discover the source of the Nile River, they traversed much of the interior of Africa in the mid- to late 1800s.

The widespread tropical diseases and fevers of Africa were the greatest challenge for explorers of the continent. The major problems were African trypanosomiasis, malaria, and yellow fever. Stanley and Livingstone were familiar with sleeping sickness (as trypanosomiasis is sometimes called) in humans and its counterpart, nagana, in cattle. They learned about the diseases from the native population and from observations they made during their travels. To avoid contracting these life-threatening illnesses, early foreign traders often stayed along the coast, where disease-carrying insects were less abundant and ocean breezes offered some relief from the biting. Explorers and missionaries who did venture into central Africa frequently died. If they survived they often suffered from lingering sickness and fevers. Livingstone himself contracted malaria and experienced declining health during his travels.

In the latter part of the 19th century, people learned more about the causes and transmission of infectious diseases. Insects were found to harbor some infectious microorganisms, which they transferred them to humans by biting. This knowledge of vectors of disease provided a basis for precautions that could somewhat lessen the risk of infection. Ultimately the desire for colonization led to some penetration into the interior of Africa by explorers from other countries. However, even today, large areas that have heavy infestations of the tsetse flies that transmit trypanosomiasis are largely unpopulated. Distribution of these insects depends on local environmental conditions within the tsetse fly belt of Central Africa. It is difficult for man and domesticated animals to survive, particularly during periods when infective vectors increase and an **epidemi**c is at hand.

THE DISEASE IN ANIMALS

It is natural for people to be concerned about their health and the effect of infectious diseases. We all hope that vaccinations, good healthful habits, and access to quality medical care will be beneficial. Many people may be unaware, however, that all living organisms, no matter how small, share a similar problem, as explained in this short poem:

> Great fleas have little fleas
> Upon their backs to bite 'em
> And little fleas have lesser fleas,
> And so ad infinitum .... [2]
>
> —Augustus De Morgan

In the microbe world, larger predatory protozoa regularly consume their bacteria prey whole, just as a frog snaps up an insect whole out of the air. It may be surprising to learn that bacteria have even smaller microbes that attack them. These microbes, called **bacteriophages**, are categorized with viruses. These organisms attach to the outside wall of a bacterium, inject their genetic material, and force the host cell to produce more bacteriophage particles. When the bacterial cell has done its work and is filled to capacity, it bursts and releases new bacteriophages that can go on to infect others. In turn all plants and animals, both predator and prey, are subject to attack by invisible microbes, just as humans are.

Trypanosomes do not infect humans exclusively. They also infect other animals, often causing anemia, diarrhea, fever, and eventually death. One group of this reservoir of animals—mammals—can carry the parasite that infects humans. However numerous animals, including some birds, reptiles, and fish, also have specific species of trypanosomes that only cause disease in those animals. African animal trypanosomiasis (AAT) affects domestic animals, including cattle, pigs, camels, goats, and sheep. Some important nonhuman species are *T. congolense*, *T. vivax*, and *T. brucei brucei*, which are primarily carried by tsetse flies. In these insects the parasites go though a life cycle and multiply. Sometimes other biting flies can transfer enough blood from an infected animal to a healthy one to cause disease, but the flies are not considered the true vectors because they do not host the parasite life cycle. Since horse and deer flies are carriers of *T. evansi*, which affects camels, horses,

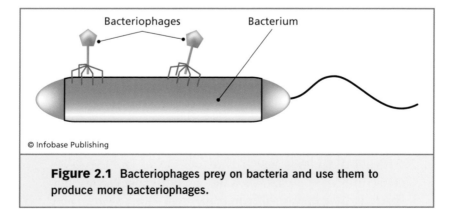

Bacteriophages   Bacterium

© Infobase Publishing

Figure 2.1 Bacteriophages prey on bacteria and use them to produce more bacteriophages.

and cattle, this disease can be found in areas outside of the tse-tse fly belt located in Central Africa. These areas include other sections of Africa as well as parts of Asia and Latin America. Likewise, horses, which are susceptible to the sexually trans-mitted *T. equiperdum,* may contract the disease in Africa as well as some areas of the Americas, Europe, and Asia. *T. vivax* is also found in South and Central America and is transmitted by bit-ing insects, while *T. evansi* can be transmitted by bats.[3] In the western United States blood from the moose, bison, pronghorn antelope, mule deer, and elk has been studied. Trypanosomes have been found to some degree in all of these species.[4]

Most trypanosome research has been conducted on human diseases and diseases that affect economically important spe-cies such as cattle. Scientists have been looking into these animal trypanosomes at least since the end of the 19th cen-tury. When more investigations are done on other species, the impact of trypanosomes on the whole animal kingdom may be more fully realized.

THE DISEASE IN HUMANS

The trypanosomes of African trypanosomiasis exist in differ-ent physical forms during their life cycle, which is explained below in more detail. The epimastigote form is found in the tsetse fly vector while the **trypomastigote** is found in human hosts. It is highly motile by flagella and is usually found in the blood. Therefore it may also be called a hemoflagellate (blood flagellate).

The trypomastigote or hemoflagellate, the only stage of *T. brucei rhodesiense and T. brucei gambiense* that lives in the human host, has an initial effect on the skin and then invades the bloodstream and **lymphatic system**. Most infected indi-viduals experience **acute** generalized symptoms, including malaise, abdominal problems, headache, chills, and fever. These symptoms are similar to those of many types of infec-tious diseases and would be difficult to diagnose except for a few important factors such as a patient's recent travel to an area

Figure 2.2 Trypanosomiasis affects many types of domestic animals and livestock, which increases risk of human infection, especially in areas where humans and animals live in close contact. © AP Images

where trypanosomiasis is endemic. Eventually, if not treated, the patient may experience degrees of paralysis, tremors, delayed pain reaction, seizures, and ultimately coma and death as the microbe invades the brain. This parasite causing African trypanosomiasis is primarily carried by various species of the tsetse fly of the genus *Glossina*, and transmitted to humans by a bite. On occasion the disease may be transmitted by other means, such as **transplacental** transfer from mother to fetus.

HISTORY OF AFRICAN TRYPANOSOMIASIS

Many scientists were involved in deciphering the mysteries of African sleeping sickness, named for symptoms of lethargy, sleepiness, and even coma in advanced cases. The names of some of the pioneers are lost to history, but several individuals are given credit for major accomplishments. In the mid-19th century, Hungarian-born physician David Gruby was working in France when he observed microbes in the blood of a frog and named them trypanosomes. British physician Joseph Everett Dutton later observed similar organisms from a human patient in Gambia, Africa, and named them *Trypanosoma gambiense*. However, it was Sir David Bruce, a pathologist from Scotland, working toward the end of the 19th and beginning of the 20th centuries, who did the most to explain the life cycle of African trypanosomiasis. The species name of the organism now bears his name (*brucei*). In demonstrating that the same trypanosome occurred in both the insect vector and the patient, Bruce showed how humans contracted the disease through an insect bite. It was a unique discovery to show that an insect harbored a protozoan parasite pathogenic for man.

Ronald Ross, a Scottish physician who had worked with malaria in the late 19th century, studied patients with sleeping sickness in the early 20th century. He was particularly interested in **periodicity** of patients' fevers and recorded fluctuations of fever throughout the illness. In the blood of patients, he examined the fascinating wiggling forms of trypanosomes among the red blood cells. Charles Louis Alphonse Laveran of France, who

AFRICAN TRYPANOSOMIASIS IN TOURISTS

African trypanosomiasis is rarely reported outside the continent of Africa, where it is endemic. However, world travelers, especially those who go on safari in East Africa, may be bitten by the tsetse fly and develop symptoms after they return to their home countries. This is uncommon, but it has been happening with more frequency lately because more people are taking exotic vacations. It is common practice in hospitals to obtain a patient history, including information on recent trips out of the country. A visit to Africa should alert the physician to the possibility of malaria or trypanosomiasis.

won the Nobel Prize in 1907, is given credit for his research with protozoan diseases. His biography and Nobel literature can be found on the Web site Nobelprize.org. Although he was not the original discoverer of the cause of African trypanosomiasis, he investigated a wide range of trypanosomes causing disease in animals and man. He studied their physical features and susceptibility to chemicals. His work and publications contributed a lot of new knowledge concerning the trypanosomes and their role in disease.

OCCURRENCE OF AFRICAN SLEEPING SICKNESS

African trypanosomiasis is prevalent on the continent of Africa between the latitudes of 15° north and 20° south. This zone encompasses a very large area of the sub-Saharan region and includes approximately 35 or more countries. *T. brucei gambiense* is found in the west and central areas, while *T. brucei rhodesiense* is found in East Africa. The tsetse fly thrives in the ecosystems of both East and West Africa. A reservoir of infected animals also exists in the area, creating an environment suitable for continuing human infections.

General Life Cycle

The life cycles of *T. brucei gambiense* and *T. brucei rhodesiense* follow the same pattern of infection from vector to host and back. A diagram (Figure 2.3) allows us to visualize what is happening in the insect, the host, and the environment as they interact. The right side of the diagram shows the parasite in a human (Steps 1–4) from the time of a bite by the infective tsetse fly (1) to the advanced disease (4). The left side illustrates developmental stages of the parasite, which occur in the tsetse fly (Steps 5–8) from the time the fly bites an infected person (5) until the mature trypomastigotes are ready to infect another person (8). Notice the symbols that show which stages are infective to humans (i) and which are used to diagnose the disease (d). Approximately 10 species of tsetse fly in two major classification groups (both male and female) are known to

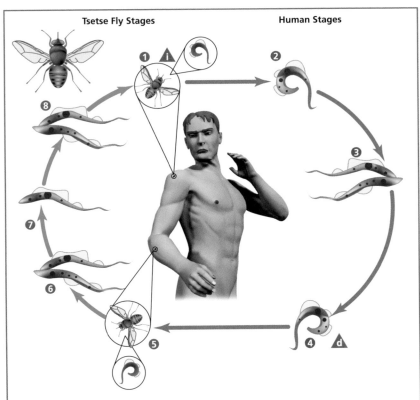

Tsetse Fly Stages

Human Stages

❶ Tsetse fly takes a blood meal (injects metacyclic trypomastigotes).

❷ Injected metacyclic trypomastigotes transform into bloodstream trypomastigotes, which are carried to other sites.

❸ Trypomastigotes multiply by binary fission in various body fluids, e.g., blood, lymph, and spinal fluid.

❹ Trypomastigotes in blood.

❺ Tsetse fly takes a blood meal (bloodstream trypomastigotes are ingested).

❻ Bloodstream trypomastigotes transform into procyclic trypomastigotes in tsetse fly's midgut. Procyclic trypomastigotes multiply by binary fission.

❼ Procyclic trypomastigotes leave the midgut and transform into epimastigotes.

❽ Epimastigotes multiply in salivary gland. They transform into metacyclic trypomastigotes.

⚠️ Infective stage   🔺d Diagnostic stage

© Infobase Publishing

Figure 2.3 The life cycle of *Trypansoma brucei* includes key developmental stages that occur within a tsetse fly. Once infected, humans and some animals become a source for further transmission of the disease.

cause trypanosomiasis. The disease is endemic over a large area of Africa but it can become epidemic depending on several factors. These include the **virulence** of the strain, the number of infective flies in an area, and the number of contacts between vector and host, or the number of people bitten in a certain time period.

Subspecies of *Trypanosoma brucei*

T. brucei rhodesiense and *T. brucei gambiense* are two subspecies of *T. brucei* found in two different locations of Africa. They are the only two subspecies that affect humans. They are both in the genus *Trypanosoma* and in the species *brucei*, but have some differences, noted in Table 2.1, that cause different clinical diseases. *T. brucei rhodesiense* is found in East Africa and the tsetse flies responsible for transmission are found in a biological category called the *Glossina morsitans* group. This group contains similar species capable of carrying trypanosomes. Hoofed animals of the savannah, such as antelope and domesticated cattle, are the main reservoirs. The disease caused by this subspecies is generally more acute than the West African variety. The tsetse flies breed in thickets and woodlands of the savanna and in the brush around Lake Victoria. *T. brucei gambiense* is found in West and Central Africa where the *Glossina palpalus* group of tsetse flies harbors the parasite. These flies live in dense vegetation near rivers and in forests. Humans are the main reservoir of infection here. Tsetse flies bite infected people, then infect other individuals.

Tsetse flies are brown, about the size of houseflies, and live only in Africa. The sleeping sickness trypanosome parasite is adapted to the insects and must go through a life cycle within the flies to continue an efficient cycle of transmission. Species and numbers of tsetse flies vary across the entire fly belt, primarily due to regional differences in temperature, rainfall, and type of vegetation. The flies' numbers may also fluctuate seasonally. Vegetation near water is the tsetse flies'

Table 2.1 Characteristics of East and West African Trypanosomiasis

Characteristic	East African	West African
Organism	*Trypanosoma brucei rhodesiense*	*Trypanosoma brucei gambiense*
Vectors	Tsetse fly, *Glossina morsitans* group	Tsetse fly, *Glossina palpalis* group
Primary Reservoirs	Animals	Humans
Illness	Acute (early CNS invasion), < 9 months	Chronic (late CNS invasions), months to years
Lymphadenopathy	Minimal	Prominent
Parasitemia	High	Low
Epidemiology	Anthropozoonosis, game parks	Anthroponosis, rural populations
Diagnostic stage	Trypomastigote	Trypomastigote
Recommended specimens	Chancre aspirate, lymph node aspirate, blood, CSF	Chancre aspirate, lymph node aspirate, blood, CSF

Source: Garcia, Lynne S., and David A. Bruckner. *Diagnostic Medical Parasitology,* Second Edition. Washington, D.C.: American Society for Microbiology, 1993.

natural habitat for breeding and survival. When the flies feed, they inject saliva, containing anticoagulants needed to keep blood flowing, into their prey. Trypomastigotes are transferred with the saliva as well.

3

Overview of American Trypanosomiasis a.k.a. Chagas' Disease

While in my garden, I noticed bits of blue and red in a bush. On closer examination, the blend of colors came from several insects clustered around an unfortunate spider. The nymphs of assassin bugs, as they turned out to be, had ambushed the spider and pierced its body with their sharp rostrums, or curved beaks. After injecting a digestive enzyme, the bugs were sucking out the fluid contents of the spider. These bugs, which are part of the order Hemiptera, are in the same family, Reduviidae, as conenose bugs and seem to share the same method of attacking prey. However, the conenose bug is known not only for its bite, but also for the dangerous parasites it carries—trypanosomes.

THE CONENOSE BUG

The conenose bug (also called triatomine bug, assassin bug, kissing bug, reduviid bug, *vinchucas* (Spanish), or *barbeiros* (Portuguese)) is an insect about 0.75 inches (1.9 cm) to over 1 inch (2.5 cm) long. Most commonly they have orange or yellow bands along their abdomen. It has a long, piercing "beak" which folds back under the head when it is not in use. There are many different species of these bugs.

This insect is called a *conenose* because it has a long, narrow head, but it is also known as a kissing bug. This is because it tends to sneak up on sleeping people and bite them on the face near the lips. These insects want to pick a spot to bite that has plenty of warm blood. The exposed face is just right for this, and the deed can be done without waking the victim.

These blood-sucking insects attack not only humans but also many other types of mammals. They live close to their victims and take a blood meal whenever they are hungry. The eastern blood-sucking conenose, *Triatoma sanguisuga,* is one conenose bug that attacks mammals for blood and is found in the eastern and southern United States. Females lay eggs after a meal and the immature nymphs soon hatch out. In the one to two years as immature nymphs, they are just as aggressive as adults. A bite from a nymph or an adult may produce severe allergic reactions in humans. The skin at the infection site becomes red and inflamed, sometimes for several weeks.

There are other species of conenose bugs in the United States. In some places conenose bugs are as abundant as

Figure 3.1 Nicknamed the "kissing bug" for its tendency to bite the face or mouth area, the conenose bug is a key vector for trypanosomiasis in South America. © Ray Coleman / Photo Researchers, Inc.

cockroaches and as difficult to keep out of the house. Close to the Mexican border, Arizona has four separate conenose species. There, the bug often lives close to its intended victim, the packrat, usually in its nest. This mammal is a curious rodent that collects all sorts of extraneous materials to add to its large, decorated nest. The bugs normally like to stay there. However, if they get inside a house, they will search for a blood meal at night. Since their beak (a term used to describe the pointed feeding tube that looks like a bird's beak) is very sharp and the bite is painless, most people do not know they have been bitten until an allergic reaction takes place. If trypanosomes are present in the excreted feces of a conenose bug, rubbing and scratching will increase the chances of introducing them from the skin into the wound and then into bloodstream.

Although conenose bugs are capable of transmitting trypanosomiasis in the United States, cases of it happening have rarely been documented. Only five cases of trypanosomiasis acquired by the bite of an assassin bug were documented in this country up to 1999.[5] However, physicians are not accustomed to looking for this disease and there may actually be more cases than people realize. The hidden **chronic** condition, instead of acute disease, is often the situation. Symptoms may develop over decades and are difficult to diagnose if American trypanosomiasis is not suspected.

American Trypanosomiasis, or Chagas' disease, is more prevalent from Mexico to the southern tip of South America and can be transmitted by several species of bugs from the genera *Triatoma*, *Rhodnius*, and *Panstrongylus*. In some areas the conenose bug lives primarily in houses while in other areas it is normally a forest-dweller. People who live near rain forests, usually farmers and other rural residents, normally live in close proximity to their domestic animals. These animals may become infected not only by bites, but also by feeding on contaminated food. The infected animals then give the insects a pool of trypanosomes. Once they pick up the trypanosomes, the bugs remain contaminated for the entire one to two years

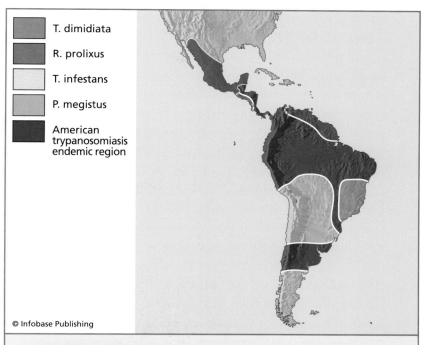

■	T. dimidiata
■	R. prolixus
□	T. infestans
▨	P. megistus
■	American trypanosomiasis endemic region

© Infobase Publishing

Figure 3.2 Four different species of conenose bugs distributed throughout South America play a major part in the transmission of trypanosomiasis. Other species of these bugs are involved to a lesser degree

of their lives. They can easily transfer these parasites to nearby humans. Thatched roofs common in these areas provide a good habitat for these insects and as a result there is a steady shower of waste products from the bugs falling into the dwelling. This can be as much of a hazard as the bug's bite, because the faces of sleeping people can become covered by debris laden with trypanosomes. Scratching or rubbing the eyes can introduce those trypanosomes into the body, allowing the disease to take hold.

AMERICAN TRYPANOSOMIASIS—THE DISEASE

American trypanosomiasis, or Chagas' disease, affects an estimated 15 to 18 million people at any time. It may be acute and lead to death unless treated or, more commonly, it can become chronic. In this long-term state, multiple tissues and organs may be involved, including the skin, skeletal muscle, lymphoid tissue, heart, esophagus, colon, and brain. Acute symptoms include enlarged lymph nodes, fatigue, fever, and swelling of one eye. In the long-term stage, 10 to 30 years after infection, patients may develop cardiac problems such as congestive heart failure, enlarged or swollen esophagus, and irregular or rapid heartbeat. This disease is transmitted primarily through the bite of a contaminated insect or accidental insertion of insect feces into the eye, mucous membranes, or broken skin. It can also be transmitted by blood transfusion, organ transplantation, during a laboratory accident while working with live trypanosomes, and from mother to fetus (**congenital** infection). A 2005 epidemic in Brazil was caused by drinking contaminated cane juice, a popular beverage.[6] Kissing bugs and feces were apparently ground up with the sugarcane during processing, which was done without pasteurization.

HISTORY OF AMERICAN TRYPANOSOMIASIS

Although American trypanosomiasis has been around for centuries, it was not until 1909 that Brazilian physician Carlos Chagas investigated the disease. He found the microbe responsible for American trypanosomiasis and learned the life cycle of infection. Because of his achievement, the disease he researched is often called Chagas' disease, in his honor.

The Work of Dr. Carlos Chagas

Dr. Carlos Chagas was born in 1879 in Oliveira, Brazil. He studied medicine at a time when malaria was rampant in his country. At first Dr. Chagas worked to help limit epidemics of malaria. He was somewhat successful in developing prevention methods that targeted the mosquito vector, such as killing mosquitoes in and around residences. While on assignment in a rural area, he heard stories about conenose bugs and their habit of biting people on the face as they slept.

Figure 3.3 Consumption of contaminated sugar cane or sugar cane juice can lead to trypanosomiasis. © Angus Plummer / iStockphoto

He decided to investigate the possibility of disease transmission. He looked first at the conenose bugs and under a microscope he observed squirming flagellates (trypanosomes) from the insects' hindgut. This established that there was a microbe

UNUSUAL EPIDEMIC OF AMERICAN TRYPANOSOMIASIS

The most common ways to get American trypanosomiasis involve the introduction of live trypanosomes into the bloodstream through a break in the skin or by blood transfusion. Since these types of transmission appear to be similar to those seen with other blood-borne infections, such as hepatitis B, it may seem unusual that ingesting bugs or their feces can also produce the disease. Somehow the trypanosomes can survive in the acidic environment of the stomach and move from the intestinal tract into the bloodstream. This may happen rarely from time to time in the endemic area, but when an epidemic takes place, it is news, as seen with the Brazil epidemic caused by contaminated cane juice. An excerpt from an article by the Science and Development Network, March 2005, is shown below:

FATAL OUTBREAK IN BRAZIL COULD STEM FROM SUGAR CANE

"Contaminated sugarcane juice is thought to be the source of a Brazilian outbreak of Chagas' disease, a potentially fatal parasitic disease normally transmitted to people by insect bites. In the past few days, health officials in the state of Santa Catarina have recorded 45 cases of patients developing symptoms of Chagas' disease after drinking the juice. At least five of the patients died. The patients initially reported having fever, migraine, and muscle pain, with some going on to develop jaundice, abdominal pain, internal bleeding, fluid in the lungs and heart failure. Blood tests confirmed the presence of *Trypanosoma cruzi*, the parasite that causes Chagas' disease, in 31 of the 45 suspected cases. The disease is usually spread to people when insects called assassin or kissing bugs bite them, but researchers believe that food and drink that have been contaminated by the parasite could be an alternative route of infection."[7]

present. Next Chagas wanted to learn if these microbes could be transferred to humans and cause an infection. To find out, he fed the trypanosomes to lab monkeys, and weeks later, the trypanosomes were found in the animals' blood. An acutely ill girl also had these same organisms in her blood, but after her symptoms went away, the trypanosomes were gone. Chagas wondered whether this meant the disease was gone or whether it had simply entered a chronic condition in which *T. cruzi* was no longer visible. Later, when studying clinical aspects of American trypanosomiasis in humans, he reported long-term chronic effects on the nervous system, heart, and digestive system, including the loss of some nerve function in several vital organs, heart failure, and enlargement of the esophagus and colon. Description of the entire life cycle of a parasitic disease is a great achievement for one person to accomplish and is summarized in this quote: "The genius of Carlos Chagas enabled him to describe, when he was only 29 years old, the agent, vectors, clinical signs in human beings, animals and the existence of animal reservoirs of a new disease which was now known as Chagas' disease ... or American Trypanosomiasis."[8]

OCCURRENCE OF AMERICAN TRYPANOSOMIASIS

American trypanosomiasis is common in Central and South America from Mexico to Argentina. This area has all the proper conditions for making the disease endemic. The environment favors the survival of many species of triatomines that are capable of carrying *T. cruzi*. These bugs thrive among millions of rural people. Brazil and Chile have had success in vector control by using insecticides. These countries' rates of transmission are quite low (less than 1 percent for young children) in comparison with much of South America.[9] American trypanosomiasis has been known as a rural disease in the past. However, with the advent of blood transfusions and the development of semirural, impoverished areas around cities, it can now be called an urban disease as well.

In the southern United States, there have been five proven vector-borne cases: Texas (three between 1955 and 1983), California (one in 1982), and Tennessee (one in 1998).[10] In addition, there have been three transplant infections from a single donor in the United States and fewer than 10 documented blood transfusion cases in both the United States and Canada.[11,12] Some immigrants who come from the major endemic area (Central and South America) as well as many small mammals in the southern United States carry *T. cruzi*, but there have still only been a few cases. Why is this so? Scientists are uncertain, but a few possibilities have been suggested. Most pertain to the conenose bug vector. In South and Central America many rural people still live in thatched, mud, or adobe huts. Crevices in these structures provide a hiding place for contaminated bugs. People who live in these places are more often exposed to bites, which increase their chances of infection. Housing in the rural United States, on the other hand, generally does not provide as many places for insects to hide. Also, it appears that the varieties of conenose bugs in the U.S. do not always follow the habit of emptying their hindgut contents right after biting. Since the infective trypanosomes are in the feces and not in the saliva, there is less opportunity for transmission.

General Life Cycle and Comparisons

All the information learned so far may be summarized in chart form. Figure 3.4 shows the complete life cycle of *T. cruzi* in the host (Steps 1–4) and in the vector (Steps 5–8). An insect with trypanosomes bites a human, who then becomes infected. The next insect to take some blood from this human also becomes infected. Now if another person is bitten, the transmission between human and insect goes on and on. The cycle involves different forms of the parasite in human host and insect vector. Notice that in American trypanosomiasis a second form (the amastigote) exists in various tissues of the body. This is in addition to the blood from a trypomastigote. The diagram shows which ones are

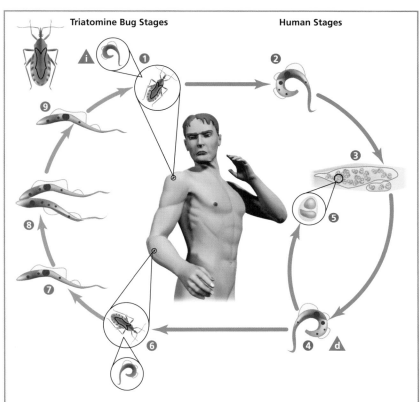

Triatomine Bug Stages   Human Stages

① Triatomine bug takes a blood meal (passes metacyclic trypomastigotes in feces, trypomastigotes enter bite wound or mucosal membranes, such as the conjunctiva).

② Metacyclic trypomastigotes penetrate various cells at bite wound site. Inside cells they transform into amastigotes.

③ Amastigotes multiply by binary fission in cells of infected tissues.

④ Intracellular amastigotes transform into trypomastigotes, then burst out of the cell and enter the bloodstream.

⑤ Trypomastigotes can infect other cells and transform into intracellular amastigotes in new infection sites. Clinical manifestations can result from this infective cycle.

⑥ Triatomine bug takes a blood meal (tripomastigotes ingested).

⑦ Epimastigotes in midgut.

⑧ Multiply in midgut.

⑨ Metacyclic trypomastigotes in hindgut.

ⓘ Infective stage   ⓓ Diagnostic stage

© Infobase Publishing

Figure 3.4 The life cycle of *Trypansoma cruzi* includes key developmental stages which occur within the midgut of a cone-nose bug. Once infected, humans and animals become a source for further transmission of the disease.

infective (i) and those used to diagnose the disease (d). It is obvious that there is a true cycle going from beginning to an endpoint and back to the beginning again. In this way, the infection by these parasites will continue as it has for thousands of years unless somehow the chain of events is interrupted.

AFRICAN TRYPANOSOMIASIS AND AMERICAN TRYPANOSOMIASIS COMPARED

Besides occurring on two different continents and being two separate species in the genus Trypanosoma, *T. brucei rhodesiense, T. brucei gambiense* and *T. cruzi* have other major differences. *T. cruzi* has a completely different insect vector, the conenose bug, and resulting disease syndrome. Although some trypomastigotes do appear in the bloodstream, **intracellular** amastigotes are the main stage in the more common chronic form. Extracellular trypomastigotes, primarily in the blood stream, are the only forms found in *T. brucei rhodesiense* and *T. brucei gambiense* infections.

As you can see, there are real differences between the diseases caused by *T. brucei rhodesiense* or *T. brucei gambiense* and *T. cruzi*. Table 3.1 summarizes these for reference.

Table 3.1 Comparison of Two Diseases

	Trypanosoma cruzi	*Trypanosoma brucei rhodesiense,* *Trypanosoma brucei gambiense*
Common name	American trypanosomiasis (Chagas' disease)	African trypanosomiasis (African sleeping sickness)
Continent	South America	Africa
Primary reservoirs	Animals	Animals in East Africa Humans in West Africa
Vector	Kissing bug	Tsetse fly
DIAGNOSTIC STAGE		
Blood	Trypomastigote	Trypomastigote
Tissue	Amastigote	Trypomastigote (if present)
Recommended specimens	Blood, lymph node aspirate, chagoma aspirate, tissue	Blood, lymph node aspirate, chancre aspirate, spinal fluid

4

A Close Look at Trypanosomes and Related Flagellates

Camping in the great outdoors is an invigorating experience. However, it is important to make sanitation, including clean drinking water, an integral part of the planning. Sickness can quickly ruin a vacation. A stream in the wilderness may look clear, but can make people ill. Even in areas far away from human habitation, wildlife may contaminate the water with infectious organisms. Beavers, in particular, carry a parasite known as *Giardia lamblia*. This is a flagellated protozoan, like the trypanosomes, but with very different physical characteristics, life cycle, and disease transmission. First in a close look, the characteristics of the trypanosomes will be explored. Then other flagellates, including *Giardia lamblia*, will be compared at the end of the chapter.

THE PHYSICAL CHARACTERISTICS OF TRYPANOSOMES

The trypanosomes of *Trypanosoma brucei* and *Trypanosoma cruzi* are long and crescent-shaped when viewed through a microscope. They range in size from 20 to 40 micrometers (a micrometer is one-millionth of a meter). There are some subtle differences between them, but they look basically the same, except that *T. cruzi* often takes the shape of the letter C on stained slides. The single flagellum at one end (of a live trypanosome) causes a snake-like motion of the entire cell. The rise and fall of a filmy structure, known as an **undulating membrane**, may also be visible under some conditions (see Figure 4.1). This membrane arises from an organelle called a

kinetoplast at the rear of the organism. From there it extends forward, attached along the edge, and finally becomes the free flagellum at the front. The whole trypanosome is duplicated by **asexual reproduction**. The single cell produces another cell of the same kind by dividing lengthwise. This would be something like cutting a banana from tip to tip the long way and having both halves form into two new, whole pieces of fruit. This division and reproduction process is called **binary fission**.

DIFFERENT FORMS IN THE TRYPANOSOMIASIS LIFE CYCLE

Trypanosomes of the type shown in Figure 4.2 are those that appear in fluids in both American and African trypanosomiasis. It is called the trypomastigote stage, has a flagellum for locomotion, and is the only form of the parasite present in *T. brucei rhodesiense* and *T. brucei gambiense* infections. American trypanosomiasis patients also have this flagellated form in the bloodstream part of the time. However there is another form of *T. cruzi* when the parasite resides inside human cells instead of the bloodstream. This is a rounder structure that has no means of locomotion and is called an **amastigote** It

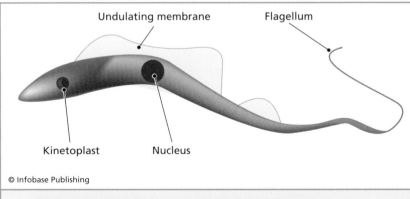

Undulating membrane   Flagellum

Kinetoplast   Nucleus

© Infobase Publishing

Figure 4.1 Different species of human trypanosomes (trypomastigote stage) vary in size and internal structure, but share a common appearance and structure.

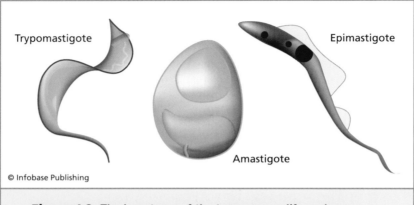

Trypomastigote

Epimastigote

Amastigote

© Infobase Publishing

Figure 4.2 The key stages of the trypanosome life cycle are trypomastigote, amastigote, and epimastogote.

resides clustered in **cysts** in affected cells. When this form is released into the blood, it again is a trypomastigote stage with a flagellum. It then moves within the body to search for other tissue or nerve cells to invade. Once inside a cell it reverts to the amastigote stage.

When a tsetse fly or conenose bug takes a blood meal, the trypomastigotes undergo a transformation to become epimastigotes (a stage only found in insects) and then back to an infective metacyclic trypomastigote. There is also multiplication of these trypomastigotes, which results in a large number of parasites available for host infection. This flagellated form, found in the salivary glands of the tsetse fly and the hindgut of the conenose bug, is ready to start another infection when the insect delivers it inside the host. The natural cycle in insects is necessary for continued transmission of these diseases to humans and animals in nature. The full life cycles of the two forms of Trypanosomiasis are shown in Chapters 2 and 3. Knowing the physical characteristics of a microbe is a good starting point, but the microbiologist must first be able to locate the infectious organism from a patient specimen. Proper laboratory techniques are necessary to maximize the chances for success.

TRYPANOSOMES AND THE IMMUNE SYSTEM

The human immune system provides amazing protection against invading microbes. Different components work together to attack viruses, bacteria, fungi, protozoa, and pathogenic worms. Protozoa parasites, like some other microbes, have developed different ways to counteract the immune system. Their life cycle involves living inside the host for a relatively long time as they obtain the energy they need to grow and reproduce. While living inside a host, parasites must evade the host's immune system if they are to survive. In some cases, parasites can avoid being destroyed by the immune system for years, as is the case with chronic American trypanosomiasis. To hide from the immune system *T. cruzi* has a second form, the amastigote stage. In this stage the trypanosome lives inside cells, where it divides and has some degree of protection from the immune system. Eventually the amastigotes change to flagellated forms that go out into the bloodstream temporarily, until they can find fresh cells to invade.

On the African continent, *T. brucei Rhodesiense and T. brucei Gambiense,* the agents that cause African sleeping sickness, travel freely in the bloodstream, because they have their own way of fooling the immune system of the host. When the body's defenses meet the trypanosomes, they zero in on the outer layer of the microbe. The human immune system makes antibodies against this outer **glycoprotein** coat and launches an attack. Many of the trypanosomes are killed. But before the antibodies can dispose of all of them, a few of the reproduced parasites have appeared with changed surfaces and are able to survive the assault. These survivors can then multiply very rapidly and invade other areas of the body before new antibodies can be made to fight them. This happens over and over again until the immune system is exhausted and the trypanosomes are able to invade the brain. At this point, the patient dies unless treated properly.

OTHER FLAGELLATES OF MEDICAL IMPORTANCE

Three other flagellates—*Giardia lamblia, Leishmania,* and *Trichomonas vaginalis*—are similar to trypanosomes, but each one has a distinct life cycle.

Giardiasis

Giardiasis is caused by the water parasite *Giardia lamblia,* found worldwide. The disease may be contracted from infective cysts

MICROSCOPIC TECHNIQUES FOR AN UP-CLOSE LOOK

Trying to find a microbe through a microscope takes practice and patience. It is not only a matter of mastering the instrument, but first preparing a proper slide for the best observation of the organism. The wet preparation is used to look at living organisms that are usually fairly large and motile. Searching for a flagellated protozoan, including a trypanosome, in a patient's body fluid is a good application for this simple technique. After a drop of the fluid is placed on a clean slide, a coverslip (a thin rectangular or square piece of glass) is placed over the drop to flatten and contain it. The slide is then placed on the stage of the microscope and the observer looks under reduced light, which reduces glare. A jerky motion will alert the microbiologist to look closer at the finer details of the microbe. A drop of blood examined this way will reveal moving trypanosomes if present in a patient specimen.

A stained slide is used to find smaller organisms such as bacteria or to observe special details in larger ones. Numerous stains are used in the laboratory for a variety of applications. One of the most common for bacteria is the gram stain. A drop of specimen is placed on a slide, allowed to dry, and then heated slightly to make the microbes stick to the slide. Next a series of staining liquids is applied, rinsed, and dried. The end result will be bacteria stained either purple (called gram posi-

in the environment, food, or directly from another person. Unsanitary and crowded conditions, especially in day care centers, prisons, and nursing homes, contribute to rapid spread and epidemics.

In the environment, *Giardia* exists as a football-shaped, very tough cyst, which can survive for long periods of time and remain infectious. After the cyst is ingested and reaches the small intestine, it turns into a fragile **trophozoite** stage that

tive) or a pink (called gram negative). Looking at the color, as well as the shape, gives a good indication of what type of organism the person is observing. Round or coccoid staph organisms stain purple and often appear in grape-like clusters. On the other hand, *E. coli* is rod-shaped, stains pink and will be separated from neighboring cells. The best stain to use for trypanosomes is a giemsa stain, which shows different structures, such as the shape of the cell, the nucleus, and the kinetoplast.

For microbes that do not stain well or are too thin to see by stain, microbiologists employ the dark field technique. A special attachment provides light from the side rather than the bottom as usual. The effect is to have a complete black background, with the moving organisms shining out brightly. This method is also applicable for trypanosomes. Another interesting way to find microbes is similar to the dark field method. Once again the background is dark, but the organisms shine out with a fluorescent apple green or yellow light from dye molecules attached to antibodies specific for the microbe being sought. If the microbes are present on the slide, the antibodies with dye will be fixed on them. When ultraviolet light strikes these organisms, a green fluorescent image appears. The microbes shine out against a black background and are easy to find.

moves by means of flagella. There it remains free or attaches with a sort of sucker disk to the intestine wall and extracts nutrients from the host. An infection with many trophozoites may produce abdominal problems including profuse diarrhea. Through a microscope, these trophozoites appear heart or pear shaped, have two large nuclei on each side, and seem to have faces with large eyes looking out. When Cortez invaded the Aztec empire in Mexico (1519), the Spaniards first encountered *Giardia lamblia.* Montezuma was the Aztec ruler at the time, and so the disease came to be known as *Montezuma's revenge.*

The related flagellates *Trypanosoma brucei* and *Trypanosoma cruzi* do not have a cyst stage and cannot survive in the environment alone. They only have the trophozoite stage that cycles back and forth between the insect vector and animal host.

Trichomoniasis

Trichomoniasis, caused by *Trichomonas vaginalis,* is passed directly from person to person. It is a genitourinary infection classified as an **STD** (sexually transmitted disease). The flagellated protozoan may cause vaginitis, urethritis, and cystitis in women and urethritis or prostatitis in men. It can be found on every continent and can cause acute symptoms or be asymptomatic. Direct observation of the trophozoites is one method of diagnosis. The parasite moves with a jerky motion and is easily seen in a wet preparation. The organism has an undulating membrane similar to trypansomes and this structure is often visible moving like waves on the ocean. Often the microbiologist initially does not see the parasite itself, but cells and other debris being moved by a trapped microbe.

These are some of the primary human pathogens in the flagellate group of protozoa. Of course, there are many non-pathogenic flagellates in soil and water that normally feed on other microbes. These have a part in the natural cycles of life on Earth and are normally harmless to man.

LEISHMANIASIS

Leishmaniasis, a protozoan parasitic disease, affects approximately 12 million people around the world. It is caused by several species of the genus *Leishmania* and is in the same family as *Trypanosoma cruzi* and *Trypanosoma brucei*. It rivals the impact of trypanosomiasis. This disease is prevalent in most warm areas of the world and occurs in two forms. The cutaneous and mucosal type affects the skin and mucous membranes, while the visceral one is a systemic disease affecting internal organs. The sand fly, an insect, is a vector of the disease and carries an infective, motile promastigote stage. Although the flagellated stage does not cause pathological problems in humans, it is present in the insect vector and is injected into the host. A non-motile amastigote stage predominates in the host cells and is carried in the macrophages (a type of white blood cell). It is called an intracellular parasite since this is the way it persists in the affected person or other mammal. Diagnosis can be made by looking for the amastigotes microscopically or growing the promastigotes (the stage in insects) and looking for the motile forms. The major species includes *L. tropica, L. major, L. aethiopica, L. braziliensis, L. mexicana, L. donovani,* and *L. chagasi.* The last two commonly cause the visceral type of Leishmaniasis.

5

Epidemiology

In 1997, Andrew Makuth, the African correspondent for the *Philadelphia Enquirer*, reported on a case of African trypanosomiasis from Tambura, Sudan. Dr. Michaeleen Richer was treating 15-year-old Julianna Jima. Makuth recounted Dr. Richer's attempt to wake the frail, 62-pound girl, who opened her eyes as though she were in a trance, and described the girl's spindly limbs as "stiff as a steel-belt radial." Trypanosomiasis, or sleeping sickness, was devouring Jima's central nervous system, and without treatment she would have fallen into a coma and died.[13]

According to the World Health Organization (WHO), African trypanosomiasis has made a resurgence on the continent of Africa. There have been three major epidemics on the African continent since the late 19th century. Currently there is an upsurge of cases that some scientists consider to be an epidemic. There are at least 36 countries affected by this disease, with particularly Angola, Sudan, and the Democratic Republic of the Congo currently experiencing long-term epidemics.[14]

On the continent of South America, American trypanosomiasis is being controlled in some areas and increasing in others. Epidemiologists are working on the complex interactions of this disease as well.

EPIDEMIOLOGY AND THE CYCLES OF PARASITES

The science of **epidemiology** deals with the causes, transmission, and distribution of diseases. It helps us understand all the factors involved in the spread of disease and perhaps find a way to interrupt the cycle and prevent the occurrence of infection. Epidemiologists are trained scientists who investigate outbreaks of diseases to find causes and offer solutions. To do their job, epidemiologists must check the rate of infection, how it is spread, and what causes it. There is always a threat from emerging infectious diseases all over the world. The Centers for Disease Control and Prevention (CDC) sends epidemiologists all over the world to help stop epidemics. Sometimes they face known diseases such as the Ebola virus in Africa, but other times they must identify mysterious microbes in the United States. This was the situation when hundreds of people took ill at a 1976 convention of Legionnaires in Philadelphia. Several months later the CDC discovered that the culprit was a little known bacterium generally found in muddy water but capable of thriving in the ecosystem of the air conditioning units in big buildings.

Both African and American Trypanosomiasis have complex life cycles, which not only involve parasite and host, but other environmental factors as well. Therefore, epidemiology is closely related to the science of **ecology**, which examines living organisms in the context of everything else around them, both living and nonliving. Before looking at the epidemiology of trypanosomiasis, it is important to examine the general ecology of infectious diseases.

EPIDEMIOLOGY RELATES TO ECOLOGY

Ecology is a science that deals with the relationship between living organisms and their environment. For example a study of a fish existing in an aquatic world with other living organisms would be an exercise in ecology. The fish must respond to other life forms as well as to all the fluctuations caused by dissolved gases, temperature, salt and other minerals, ph (acidity and alkalinity), water current, and light. Every environment is a balanced ecosystem that has evolved over a long period of time. An ecosystem is similar to the physiological balance of the human body, which is called **homeostasis**. Changes may be brought into harmony or equilibrium by a system of checks and balances. This means, for example, that if the blood is too acidic or alkaline or the level of glucose (blood sugar) is too high or too low, the body can correct the situation to a normal level. However, the human body as well as the environment may suffer irreversible damage from disease, neglect, or abuse. Then the normal mechanisms to bring conditions back into balance may not work.

Organisms that cause infectious diseases, including trypanosomiasis, are also subject to fluctuations in the environment. Environmental changes may result in an increase or a decrease in incidence of disease. For example, if a healthy forest is cut down, the balance of the ecosystem is destroyed. It is possible that harmful vector species then might thrive because of more breeding sites or because controlling species that lived in the destroyed ecosystem are no longer able to survive there. Humans who venture into this area would encounter a larger number of disease-carrying insects.

Even if an ecosystem is healthy, the intrusion of humans into natural ecological cycles may be problematic. This is especially true if the ecosystem is a wilderness area not often visited by people. Africans displaced by war or famine, for example, may be forced to move to areas with heavy infestations of tsetse flies and be more vulnerable to trypanosomiasis. Some microbes in wilderness areas have made the transition from animals to man and produced diseases not seen before. These are included in the category of emerging infectious diseases—those that were absent or not as noticeable in the past, but now have made an appearance in the human population. Clearing or otherwise altering areas of the rainforest in Brazil changes ecological balance and, in some instances, has resulted in greater numbers of cases of American trypanosomiasis.[15] Changes in the environment or agricultural practices can also affect the breeding of tsetse flies and increase the likelihood of African trypanosomiasis.

EPIDEMIOLOGY OF AFRICAN TRYPANOSOMIASIS

A trypanosomiasis epidemic in Uganda, which started in the 1970s in southern areas of the country, has been spreading northward into sections where the disease was not previously a problem. Scientists concluded that an increase of tsetse flies, ample opportunity for flies to contact people, inadequate control measures, and movement of infected cattle have contributed to the epidemic.[16] In order for tsetse flies to transmit African sleeping sickness, they must first obtain a blood meal from a suitable pool of infected animals (either human or other animals). In the Gambian type of trypanosomiasis, caused by *T. brucei gambiense*, the flies get their infected blood meals mainly from humans. If not many infected humans are available for the flies to feed on, then fewer flies will be infected, and in turn, will infect fewer people through their bites. If a larger number of people have the disease, they will help keep the level of disease high. On the other hand, the reservoir of the Rhodesian type of trypanosomiasis, caused by *T. rhodesiense*, includes a wide range of animals. Domestic cattle and game animals such as antelope and bushbuck are spread over a large area, making it difficult to control the spread of the disease. In addition, there are other species of *Trypanosoma* besides *Trypanosoma brucei rhodesiense* and *Trypanosoma brucei gambiense* that infect animals of Africa. However, these do not appear to cause disease in humans even when they are present in animal populations.

Since the tsetse fly must feed on an infected person or animal in order to transfer the disease, not all flies are necessarily infected. However, both male and female flies may acquire the disease and remain infective for months. If there is a low level of infection and transmission in a specific area, the disease is called endemic. However, if changes occur, such as an increase in the reservoir population and the number of infected tsetse flies, an epidemic is likely. In this instance, the number of cases rises dramatically and may persist in this state for an extended time.

Other dynamics, besides those mentioned, might come into play to cause an outbreak. These have to do with the variables in the host, parasite, and vector. How effective a fly is can differ due to its individual makeup and behavior. This relates to factors that include the type of species, sex, age, genetic makeup, health, and ability to find hosts through visual and olfactory (odor or smell) senses.

If a new, more virulent, strain of trypanosome appears, there may be a rise in the number of cases of trypanosomiasis.

THE HUMAN ECOSYSTEM

The human body is a natural ecosystem that is home to a large number of species. It is estimated that the average person has about 10 times as many microbes as human cells in his or her body. In fact, human health often depends on the work of microbes that are collectively known as normal flora. These microbes help digest food, prevent disease-causing microbes from living in the body, and produce nutrients that help keep the body healthy. When these microbes are in balance with one another, the situation is stable. Many species exist together and control the overgrowth of the others. However, when there is a disruption, one or more species may grow very rapidly and cause problems. This is often seen with the use of antibiotics, powerful drugs that are sometimes needed to fight an infection by an unwanted pathogen. The problem arises when antibiotics have the unintended consequence of temporarily killing off a large number of the body's normal flora. A few resistant or surviving microbes, sometimes those which are part of the normal flora, can then increase greatly without competition of others that have been killed. They may cause medical problems unrelated to the infection being treated. One example is colitis, a severe intestinal problem caused by the toxin-producing bacterium *Clostridium difficile*. These bacteria may normally be present in very low numbers or may be acquired from the environment without harm. However, once *Clostridium difficile* multiplies rapidly and produces destructive toxin or poison, it has to be eradicated. It often takes a special antibiotic to restore a normal balance once again.

It may be a genetic strain that has the ability to invade the body more efficiently, or multiply faster in vector or host. It is then possible that fewer of the more pathogenic flagellates would be required to start an infection.

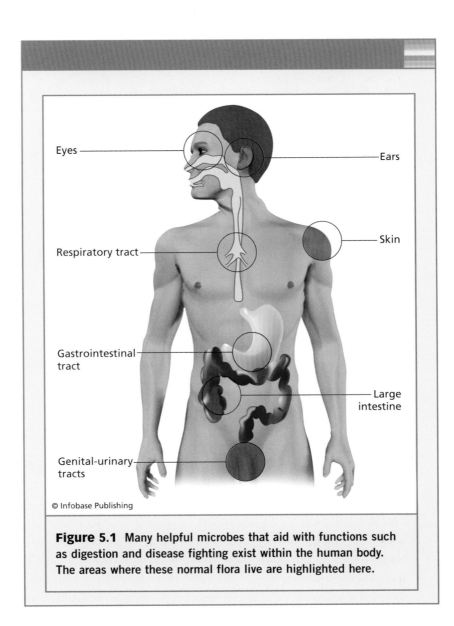

© Infobase Publishing

Figure 5.1 Many helpful microbes that aid with functions such as digestion and disease fighting exist within the human body. The areas where these normal flora live are highlighted here.

Figure 5.2 The tsetse fly is the key vector for trypanosomiasis in Africa. © AP Images

Of course the health status of the host is important, too. Every individual has his or her unique genetic makeup and immune status, or ability to fight infection. Some people are more susceptible to contracting sleeping sickness than others. Populations that have evolved in places where resident parasites are common are sometimes better able to cope with infections. Settlers from another area, however, who have never been exposed to these microbes, would be more likely to contract the disease. People with impaired immune systems and the young are generally more susceptible to trypanosomiasis and are more likely to die from these illnesses. Older individuals are often as vulnerable as children to infectious diseases. However, if older individuals have survived repeated exposures to trypanosomes, they might have some protection against the full severity of the disease.

EPIDEMIOLOGY OF AMERICAN TRYPANOSOMIASIS

Epidemiologists are studying problem areas in the fight against American trypanosomiasis, which is present in Argentina and other South American countries. However, identifying and addressing the means of transmission can be tricky and time consuming. Spraying houses there with insecticides is generally effective against the conenose bug, *Triatoma infestans*, which is the carrier of *Trypanosoma cruzi*. The bugs in one area of Argentina, though, have been reappearing sooner than expected after treatments. A recent study conducted to determine why this is happening helped scientists conclude that the bugs are not crawling from forested areas near the houses, but coming from some distance away.[17] The study found that if houses in far away communities are not treated with insecticide, some bugs will fly from there to other houses over quite a distance. This study gives health personnel a good idea how to attack the problem now. All communities must be treated in a large area to prevent reinfestation of houses by flying conenose bugs.

In the Amazon rain forest, family clusters of American trypanosomiasis disease have emerged.[18] This is not typical for the area, and contaminated food, rather than the bites of conenose bugs, is suspected in the infection transmission in these cases. More information needs to be gathered to determine what has changed and why this is happening before a plan for prevention can be started.

It is difficult to sometimes determine how an individual becomes infected. The bite of a conenose bug is probably the primary means. The bug itself may become a carrier of trypanosomes by the blood of a human or the many wild and domesticated mammals of the surrounding area. The feces of this vector, because it contains live trypanosomes, is a problem in the environment even if it is not introduced into a bite wound. Rubbing feces into the eye and mucous membranes with dirty hands is dangerous. Piercing or scratching the skin with any contaminated object, or **fomite**, might inject *T. cruzi* into the bloodstream. This could happen with a sharp twig outdoors or a broken slide in a laboratory. Consuming food that is tainted with bugs or their feces can cause infection that starts in the gastrointestinal tract. Therefore it is good practice to thoroughly wash fruits and vegetables consumed raw and use clean water. Finally, there is also a danger of transmission by blood transfusion, organ transplantation, or transfer from mother to fetus. If a rise in the number of cases occurs or the disease spreads to a different geographical area, the means of transmission may not be easy to solve.

There are large areas of South and Central America and the southern United States in which American trypanosomiasis is endemic. An epidemic can occur if conditions are right. An increase in the size of the reservoir, or the number of infected vectors, or changes in the virulence of the trypanosome are some of the factors that may cause an increase in the number of cases. It appears that the behavior of the conenose bug is also a factor. In fact, to understand this disease, the basic biology of the vector must be understood. There are some species that prefer the forest (*sylvatic* species) and others that prefer living in human dwellings. The forest species will move into houses under certain circumstances, such as alteration of their environment. Therefore migration habits of the bugs are important. Their feeding behavior determines if trypanosomes from the insect's gut will efficiently enter the bloodstream of a host after biting. This seems to vary from species to species and perhaps place to place. Lastly epidemiology has to take into account the customs of the human population. There are questions that need to be addressed. Is there something that puts the people at increased risk for the diseases? Do they recognize the means of transmission of American trypanosomiasis and take adequate precautions? Does there need to be better education in these remote areas? These and other considerations help to combat this infectious disease.

As with African trypanosomiasis, the condition of the host determines whether or not infection will occur and how severe it will be. Initially infection may depend on the number and strain of hemoflagellate that is injected. The general health, age, and genetic makeup of the patient will also determine whether the infection will be acute, **asymptomatic**, resolve without treatment, or enter a chronic phase. In many instances the chronic condition prevails and may last for rest of the individual's life. In these cases the lifespan of an infected person is shortened considerably.

A NEW METHOD FOR EPIDEMIOLOGY— SATELLITE IMAGING MAPS

In the 20th and 21st centuries, satellites have proven useful for many kinds of scientific studies. They show not only the general topographic features of the landscape on Earth, but also vegetation, animals, water resources, and the effects of human activities. The view from space is very revealing. On the last manned U.S. space mission in August 2005, commander Eileen Collins looked at Earth from space and noticed the harmful impact of human activities, including loss of vegetation and deterioration of soil cover, that were visible from space.[19]

A very valuable satellite application has been applied to infectious diseases. Geographic Information Systems and Remote Sensing are able to help in the fight against trypanosomiasis. With this technique images from space help to show and correlate the distribution of vectors, animal reservoirs, human infections within populations, and environmental factors affecting transmission of this disease. The tsetse flies that spread African sleeping sickness require a specific breeding environment. These suitable insect habitats can be identified on satellite images. The information is then used to pinpoint major areas of disease transmission for African trypanosomiasis and other diseases. PAAT (Programme Against African Trypanosomiasis) is a program by several international organizations that utilizes these techniques. Distribution of infected humans, domestic cattle, breeding sites for the tsetse fly, and other environmental factors can be detected and used for planning preventive measures. [20]

COMPARING PARASITES

Schistosomiasis is caused by worm parasites, called blood flukes, with a relatively complex life cycle. Three species infect man: *Schisotsoma japonicum, S. mansoni, and S. haemotobium.* The first two reside as paired adults in the veins of the intestines, while the latter is found in the urinary bladder. Eggs, which look different for each species, are produced and released either in the feces or urine depending on location of the breeding worms. This disease can be chronic for decades and produce severe symptoms in the host.

The natural life cycle differs from that of trypanosomiasis. It takes place in an aquatic environment once the eggs are deposited there by the host. There is no need for a vector since various stages of the worm itself can penetrate the outside of the two different animals to complete its life cycle. The forked tail cercariae is the stage that invades the skin of humans. The miracidia from the parasite eggs, on the other hand, enter snails to mature into the cercariae. In reality, the worm needs two living organisms to complete its life cycle and become infective—one is the snail, an intermediate host, and the other is a human, where the adults reside (definitive host). In some instances animals may also harbor the mature

The European Space Agency is helping in the fight against American trypanosomiasis in Nicaragua. Satellite images are being used to locate houses that might harbor kissing bugs. People on the ground then map and inspect these dwellings. If necessary, they help make the house insect-proof.[21] GIS is being used effectively in parts of South America for surveillance of conenose bug habitats in relation to areas of settlements with human cases of American trypanosomiasis. This enables personnel to determine the effectiveness of control measures.

worms. Both immature stages of the worm can survive for a time in the water until they find the appropriate host. There are many variables in the environment as well as the two hosts, which affect the transmission of the disease. When the Aswan High Dam was built in the 1960s across the Nile River in Egypt, a large reservoir formed. The slow-moving water favored an explosive growth of snails and, with it, an increase of human infections.

Waterfowl in the United States are infected by their own schistosomes, which have a similar life cycle to the human species. If humans decide to swim or wade in the same water, the cercariae also try to penetrate human skin. They do not quite make it completely in the wrong host, but do produce a rash on the skin called swimmer's itch. It is good advice to avoid swimming in an area with waterfowl.

As you have seen, the schistosomiasis (worm parasite) and trypanosomiasis (protozoan parasite) life cycles are quite different. However, they both depend on complex interrelationships that have evolved over time. In the final analysis, these parasites are each successful in their own unique ways.

6

Clinical Disease

In one of the driest places on Earth, the Atacama Desert of South America, Peruvian and Chilean Indians have buried their dead for centuries. Scientists have learned that some of these bodies are about 9,000 years old. In shallow graves the bodies became very dehydrated. The hot, arid environment, not artificial preservatives, turned the bodies into mummies. In some, **pathological** signs are present, including the features of long-term infection with *Trypanosoma cruzi*. These signs include an enlarged esophagus, colon, and inflamed heart. When the amastigotes invade cells they destroy tissue and nerves. This

Figure 6.1 The arid environment of the Atacama desert helped preserve ancient specimens of *Trypanosoma cruzi*.
© Kriando Design / iStockphoto

Figure 6.2 Evidence of *Trypanosoma cruzi* was recovered from mummies like the one seen here found in the Atacama desert.
© Francois Gohier / Photo Researchers, Inc.

results in partial paralysis of some organs, with accumulation of food in the digestive tract and inefficient bloodflow in the heart. The pressure and stagnation adds to the permanent damage of these organs. The final proof that American trypanosomiasis is an ancient disease has come from modern techniques and the work of scientists such as the **paleopathologist**. African trypanosomiasis is also a disease that has been prevalent for centuries.

PATHOGENESIS OF TRYPANOSOMIASIS— AFRICAN AND AMERICAN

It is certain that *T. cruzi, T. brucei rhodesiense,* and *T. brucei gambiense* parasites have been causing human disease for

---

THE WORK OF A PALEOPATHOLOGIST

Mystery novels and crime shows are popular forms of entertainment. The TV show *CSI:* explores the role of scientists in solving crimes, such as homicides. The forensic pathologist is an important member of this group of scientists. It is his or her job to autopsy the body of the victim to determine the cause of death. Under normal circumstances, a forensic pathologist examines the body of a person who has recently died. A specialist called a paleopathologist (*paleo-* means *old*), on the other hand, inspects ancient remains. Specimens that are thousands of years old have been found preserved in different ways: by embalming chemicals in Egyptian tombs, by the intense heat and dryness of the desert in South America, by the acidic waters of bogs, and by the constant freezing temperatures of glaciers. The purpose of examining ancient remains is to learn the accurate facts about how people lived and died a long time ago. It is intriguing to discover what diseases or other causes were responsible for their deaths. Scientists can also learn what the human lifestyles were like in different periods of history. For instance, in rare cases, remnants of the last meal can be found and analyzed.

a very long time, as paleopathologists have discovered. It is time to look at a good summary of the **pathogenesis** (development of the disease) of both American and African trypanosomiasis. A complete description of symptoms can be found in the fact sheets on the CDC (Centers for Disease Control and Prevention) Web site listed in the bibliography.

African Trypanosomiasis

The case history (on the following page) from the periodical, *Emerging Infectious Diseases*, emphasizes the nature and severity of African Trypanosomiasis.

Paleopathologists primarily use autopsy techniques to visually inspect ancient remains. Abnormal organ tissue or bones may give the visual clues, and laboratory tests provide additional information. Microscopic and other examinations are performed on tiny specimens of tissues. These may show characteristic bacteria indicating tuberculosis infection in lungs, or signs of worm parasites in intestines. Fortunately scientists now have DNA testing to help them further. After thousands of years, it is difficult to find intact DNA to work with, but sometimes tissue specimens yield important data. Traces of *T. cruzi* DNA have been found in some mummies exhibiting signs of Chagas' disease.[22] This seems to indicate that *T. cruzi* was present and produced the internal abnormalities observed.

Studies done by paleopathologists not only shed light on what has happened in the past, but this information can then be used to get a clearer understanding of what is happening at present. Historical information is always useful for a guide to what is occurring today. Hopefully this data will be of benefit to humans living now and in the future.

"A 51-year-old man returned from a 14-day game-viewing vacation in the Luangwa Valley of southern Zambia on October 11, 2000. He had been well while traveling but had sustained numerous mosquito and tsetse fly bites. Two days after his return, he noticed an enlarging, slightly tender, erythematous lesion on his right shoulder. ...Two days later he became very ill with severe generalized myalgia, abdominal discomfort, diarrhea, vomiting, headache, fever, rigors, and sweats, but did not seek medical attention. On day 10 after his return, he consulted his primary-care physician and was admitted to his local hospital. No malaria parasites were seen on a blood film, but numerous trypomastigotes of Trypanosoma were identified, confirming the diagnosis of African trypanosomiasis. ... The trypomastigotes of T. b. rhodesiense are indistinguishable morphologically from those of T. b. gambiense, but from the epidemiology of these infections the patient was presumed to have T. b. rhodesiense infection, for which the recommended initial therapy is intravenous suramin." [23]

In its early stages, African sleeping sickness produces generalized symptoms that are common to many diseases. The red sore from the tsetse fly bite and a history of residence or travel in Africa are two specific clues that trypanosomiasis may be the problem. In sleeping sickness, particularly the West African variety, swollen lymph nodes on the back of the neck, known as Winterbottom's sign, are an indication of the disease. In its later stages, African trypanosomiasis produces neurological symptoms that include confusion, problems with speech, loss of coordination, seizures, and drowsiness. The patient will often sleep for many hours, mostly during the day. This is how the disease got the name *sleeping sickness*. Despite the name, the patient often experiences periods of sleeplessness at night. Both *T. brucei gambiense* and *T. brucei rhodesiense* are eventually fatal if not treated. Deterioration

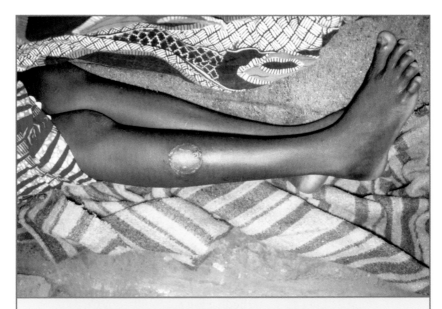

Figure 6.3 The bite of the tsetse fly leaves a distinctive chancre, an indicator used in the diagnosis of African trypanosomiasis. © Andy Crump, TDR, WHO / Photo Researchers, Inc.

of the brain is the final assault on the body. The West African form of Trypanosomiasis has a longer incubation period before severe symptoms appear.

A patient examination probably would reveal a telltale, inflamed skin lesion from the tsetse fly bite. Microscopic analysis of a blood specimen from the patient is the other major piece of the puzzle. If a microbiologist finds trypanosomes in the blood, this confirms a diagnosis of sleeping sickness. In late-stage African trypanosomiasis, these parasites may also be found in the spinal fluid. New molecular methods such as **PCR** and DNA probes are being used successfully in cases where there are fewer parasites than can be found by microscopy. These rely not only on the eyes of a microbiologist, but sometimes on machines specially designed to detect and identify traces of the microbes. The final results are presented to the microbiologist on a computer interface.

T. brucei gambiense and *T. brucei rhodesiense* must be treated with antibiotics effective against these specific protozoa to halt the progression of disease. Suramin and pentamidine are the most commonly used drugs in the early stages of the disease, while melarsoprol and eflornithine treat late stage sleeping sickness. It is important to try to stop the parasite before it reaches the spinal fluid that surrounds the brain.

American trypanosomiasis

This account from the Web site, *Kiss of Death,* illustrates the effects of a chronic case of Chagas' disease.

> "Bertha (a pseudonym) lives in La Paz, Bolivia, and her medical history provides insight into the effects of Chagas. She suffers from chronic heart ailments from Chagas' disease. As a child living the 1930s, she was bitten by *vinchucas* [conenose bugs] and infected with T. cruzi when she lived in Tupiza, a small rural village in Bolivia. … She made a living by sewing for wealthy people, but in 1974 she was diagnosed with Chagas' disease. … Until she was forty-four she was healthy, going up and down the hills of La Paz to do her sewing. In 1974 she felt fatigue. She began to get a swollen throat and spit blood. She didn't know what it was; she had no idea it had to do with the *vinchucas* bites years before. She would get tired, fatigued, and experience dizzy and fainting spells. … She continued to do her sewing though she sometimes would faint while she was working. The fainting spells continued for a year; the next year her fainting got more severe and she eventually suffered a stroke. … She underwent testing, xenodiagnosis, that indicated she had Chagas' disease. X-rays showed that she didn't suffer from cardiomegaly (an enlarged heart), but that she probably had lesions in her heart's electrical system. These were caused

by T. cruzi amastigotes being encysted in her cardiac tissue. This condition can be fatal. Dr. Jauregui implanted a pacemaker in 1980 when Bertha's heart rhythm worsened. The pacemaker keeps the heart rhythm constant and Bertha's condition improved. She was able to resume her seamstress work, although she suffered minor fatigue as she climbed the streets of La Paz at 12,000 feet."[24]

American trypanosomiasis can be acute, but most cases of the disease are chronic infections that last for several decades. The acute disease causes generalized symptoms similar to those of numerous infectious diseases. There may be fever, swelling of the lymph nodes, enlargement of the liver and spleen, general body aches, inflammation at the site of the conenose bug bite, swelling of the eye, and, in severe cases, inflammation of the heart and brain. Romaña's sign (a swelling of usually one eye) is caused by rubbing fecal trypanosomes from the conenose bug into the eye. In this acute illness, brain or cardiac symptoms may be noted in some patients. Decades after the initial infection, about one-third of patients show damage to the heart and intestinal tract from chronic infection.

WHO GETS INFECTED?

Not everyone who lives in or visits an endemic area will acquire the infective parasite and, even if they do, the disease they develop might not be severe. What determines whether you get an infection or somehow evade the disease? Why doesn't everyone who is bitten by a vector get the disease?

For an infection to take place, a person must be bitten by an insect that is carrying the parasite. This only happens when the vector had already, at least once in its life, fed on an organism that had the disease. The vector would then have to introduce a sufficient number of parasites to the new host to overwhelm the body's defenses. Some parasites are more virulent—better able to cause an infection—than others. T. brucei rhodesiense, the East African strain of sleeping sickness, causes disease with more intensity than the West

Figure 6.4 Romaña's sign usually affects one eye and indicates the presence of American trypanosomiasis.
© WHO/TDR/Wellcome

African strain, *T. brucei gambiense*. In exposure with the *gambiense* subspecies, there is also a longer lapse of time before severe symptoms develop, and the incubation period for an individual may be months to years. In the rhodesian form days to weeks are the rule.

Just as all vectors or microbes in a population are not alike, no two hosts are the same. American trypanosomiasis is more often acute when it affects children under five years of age or people whose immune systems are weakened by diseases. AIDS, for instance, increases a person's susceptibility to many infectious diseases and **opportunistic infections**. On the other hand, some people develop no symptoms at all or develop only a short illness that goes away by itself. Their immune systems are able fight off the parasites so they do not cause lasting disease. This appears to occur at times with African sleeping sickness. However, if a patient with African trypanosomiasis *does* show symptoms, the disease will become acute and eventually progress to the brain.

A chronic condition in which parasites are present but do not immediately cause extreme illness may also occur. In American trypanosomiasis, this phase is common and may last for decades before the chronic symptoms appear. During this time period, *T. cruzi* causes a great deal of irreversible damage to many organs. African trypanosomiasis is more **progressive** and does not produce a chronic condition for very long, especially in the East African subspecies. Left untreated, it will eventually involve the brain and cause death.

TARGET ORGANS

The symptoms of a disease are clues to what is happening inside the body. Both *T. brucei rhodesiense* and *T. brucei gambiense* damage the skin, the lymphatic system, **viscera**, and finally the brain. It is injury to the brain that causes coma and death.

The skin, liver, spleen, lymphatic system, and sometimes the heart and brain, may be affected in acute infection with *T. cruzi*. The chronic phase primarily damages the esophagus, colon, skeletal muscle, heart, and nerves specifically in these organs. In fact damage to the nervous system causes many of the problems associated with these organs. The nerves of the esophagus and colon become so damaged that the organs stop functioning well. This leads to difficulty swallowing and sometimes a blockage of the large intestine. In many cases surgery is needed. The heart may become enlarged and will no longer pump blood efficiently. The rhythm will often be uneven (arrhythmia) and signs of heart failure will be evident.

PREVENTION OF INFECTIONS IN LABORATORY WORKERS

There are approximately 500,000 laboratory workers in the United States who deal with pathogenic microbes. It is estimated that each year about three out of 1,000 will get a laboratory-acquired infection.[25] Bacteria and viruses cause most of these accidental infections, but fungi and parasites can produce them too. Live trypanosomes in patient specimens are considered a real risk.

Because of this problem, there are strict regulations governing safety procedures in the lab. Periodic inspections by outside agencies assure that these rules are being followed. A small, cramped area can be a hazard. Proper design of the floor space allows for efficient workflow while decreasing the chance that workers will bump into objects or other people. All employees, when they are involved in hazardous tasks, are required to wear protective equipment, such as a lab coat, gloves, and goggles. Along with personal safety gear, proper hand washing is a necessary precaution. Eating, smoking, and drinking are prohibited in the lab work area, except in special rooms set aside for these activities. Lab workers always assume that every specimen they work with is capable of causing an infection. This concept is referred to as *universal precautions* and is a good philosophy for minimizing infections. There must be adequate disinfection or sterilization of soiled objects. Any waste must be properly disposed of to reduce the chances of environmental contamination outside the laboratory.

The amastigotes living in cells cause a thinning of the walls of the heart as the tissue is destroyed. Heart attacks may occur at middle age in infected people. The patient must take numerous medications and may even require a heart transplant.

CLINICAL DIAGNOSIS—IDENTIFYING TRYPANOSOMIASIS

It can be difficult to determine the cause of an illness. To do so doctors draw on their knowledge from medical school, their experience diagnosing diseases, reference books and reputable sites on the Internet, as well as consultation with colleagues. Also, diagnostic services such as medical imaging or laboratory diagnosis are an essential part of clinical diagnosis. A blood specimen can provide many clues about the patient's condition. An infectious organism, for example, may be found when a doctor or laboratory technologist looks at a sample under a microscope. Doctors may also identify a disease by information about antibodies, which are made in response to specific diseases, in the blood. This search is an important task. It is sometimes the only way for a physician to make a diagnosis and provide the patient with appropriate treatment.

In doing their job, all medical personnel must protect themselves from any infectious agent that patients may have. The most common means of exposure include inhalation of aerosols, accidental ingestion of live organisms, inoculation of microbes into the skin, and contamination of the mucous membranes. This may happen when examining a patient or patient specimen. Live trypanosomes from an infected patient may in turn infect a healthcare worker if precautions are not taken.

7

Diagnosis in the Laboratory

In nature, some animals are easy to spot. For instance, the bright blue of an indigo bunting bird radiates from green foliage. But other animals are more difficult to detect. A camouflaged horned toad blends into the color of the desert floor, remaining almost invisible unless it moves. The shape of what the eye sees is very important also, and the brain catalogues a form from past experience and recalls what the observed object might be when it is seen again. In the same vein, microbiologists looking through a microscope observe a fascinating miniature world amid a background of extraneous material. Here too, color, motion, and shape are the keys to successfully finding microbes. Organisms are detected by motion and shape when allowed to move in a drop of liquid, while a stained slide is often necessary to differentiate organisms by artificial coloring and shape. A special instrument, the electron microscope, is necessary to capture an image of a viral particle.

IDENTIFICATION BY MICROSCOPY

Although the medical laboratory has recently incorporated many sophisticated techniques to identify microorganisms, the traditional task of looking through a light microscope at patient specimens is still important. This method is one of the quickest ways for an experienced microbiologist to provide the doctor with a diagnosis. Only then can a rapid treatment regimen be initiated. The initial question is how to diagnose trypanosomiasis by looking through a microscope. This is generally done in the laboratory by technologists and the results reported to the doctor.

74

In African trypanosomiasis, the only form of the parasite is the flagellated trypomastigote. It can be found in the blood, spinal fluid, or **aspirant** from lymph nodes, depending on the stage of disease. A drop of fluid is placed on a slide, covered by a coverslip, and then viewed under a microscope. The shape, motion, and size of the microbe help microbiologists determine which pathogen is causing the disease. With American trypanosomiasis, the acute illness may provide this rapid lab diagnosis, because the infectious organism may be found in the blood. However, during the chronic stage, there are few trypomastigotes in the blood. In this instance, most organisms are inside the cells in the amastigote stage (nonmotile). Therefore, a stained slide of the content of cells is necessary for diagnosis. Dyes are used to selectively color the substance. In this way, amastigotes, if they are present, will show up as a characteristic shape and color against the background of different-colored cellular material.

Sometimes there may be too few parasites present in the blood to find on a microscope slide. Therefore, a special method to focus the parasites at one location may be helpful. This is a bit like letting a jar of muddy water settle for a few hours. The top layer of water then can be poured off to reveal the concentrated mud particles and other debris on the bottom. In the laboratory, a **centrifuge** does the same thing by spinning the sample to concentrate particles on the bottom of a tube. There are other methods of doing this, which in some cases perform the same task better. They allow detection of lower numbers of parasites in the blood than traditional procedures. In one method, a column with a positively charged interior is used as a funnel. Because opposite charges attract, negatively charged red blood cells become trapped by the column while the positively charged trypanosomes pass through with the liquid. In this way separation is achieved and the parasites are concentrated without red cells in the contents that flow through the column.

Staining slides and the organisms on them, is a way to confirm what has been seen. This is similar to painting an object a bright color that is different from its surroundings. When one of the laboratory stains is used, certain features of microbes will stand out. In the case of trypomastigotes, the

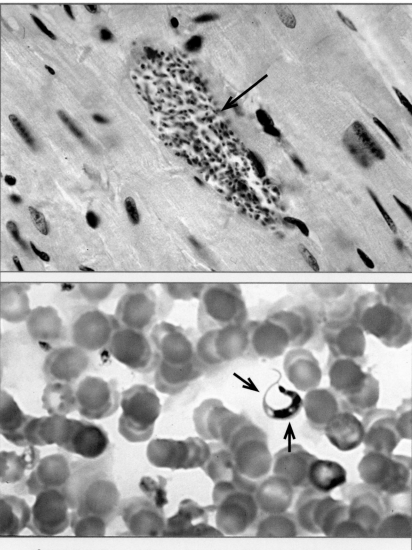

Figure 7.1 These stained microscope slides show the amastigote (above) and trypomastigote (below) of *Tryapnosoma cruzi*. © WHO/ TDR/Stammers

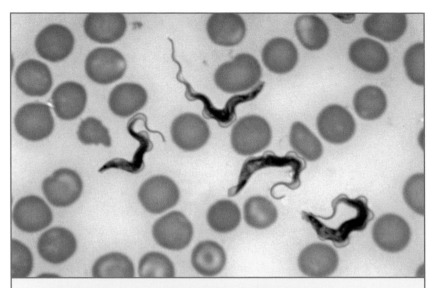

Figure 7.2 This stained microscope slide shows the trypomastigote of *Trypanosome brucei*. © WHO/TDR/Stammers

characteristics that show up are the nucleus, kinetoplast, and sometimes flagella. The trypanosomes of *T. cruzi* and *T. brucei* are different but look very similar microscopically. In the case of American trypanosomiasis, staining and shape are the only characteristics to visualize the intracellular amastigotes since they are in the cells and do not move. *T. rangeli,* an animal trypanosome that looks like *T. cruzi* in the trypomastigote form, sometimes may be present in specimens. It has not been proven to cause clinical disease but could lead a doctor to an incorrect diagnosis.

Identification by Serology

When we cannot find the organism directly under a microscope, the next best option is to find evidence that the body has been exposed to it. This is in the form of specific antibodies produced by the immune system as a defense against infectious disease. White cells, called **lymphocytes**, are found in two types. B cells exposed to **antigens** (foreign organisms) and produce protein antibodies that can be distributed throughout the body by blood. T cells work with B cells to rid the body of invaders. They send chemical signals, and one kind, a killer cell, can attach to foreign cells and destroy them. There are several types of **antibodies** also called **immunoglobulins** (IgG, IgM, IgA, IgD, and IgE), which are secreted by B cells and can be enlisted to fight various microbes. Macrophages and leukocytes are different white cells that crawl around and engulf and ingest microbes. This is similar to an amoeba feeding on food particles in the water. Antibodies are found in the blood and are distributed to all parts of the body. In patients with African trypanosomiasis, there is a large amount of IgM, which can react against the glycoprotein coat of the trypanosome in the patient's blood. IgM is usually the first antibody produced and then others take over. In acute American trypanosomiasis, IgM is also the first antibody produced, but in the long-term

DETERMINING THE SIZES OF MICROBES

To identify certain microbes correctly, we need to know their size as well as their physical characteristics. A comparison of all information with a reference book that shows pictures and sizes of parasites allows scientists to reach a correct identification. Obtaining a measurement of a microbe is not an easy task, but it can be done. Individuals are normally accustomed to measuring objects that they can see. Since almost all microbes are smaller than one millimeter, the first mark on a ruler, they require a much smaller device that uses micrometers rather than millimeters. This tiny measuring tool can be inserted permanently into the eyepiece of a microscope. Anyone who looks through the microscope will see the ruler, and then, when a slide is viewed, the ruler and microbe will be seen together. It is then easy to line them up and determine the size of the microbe.

chronic stage, IgG is produced most. Searching for this antibody may sometimes be the only way to diagnose a chronic case of American trypanosomiasis. Scientists have developed several types of tests to detect the presence of specific antibodies; all of these tests must be interpreted with caution because they are not 100 percent accurate, but they remain quite useful in helping doctors reach a diagnosis.

Other Methods for Diagnosing Trypanosomiasis

Cultures (growths of live microbes) of bacteria and fungi in agar petri plates have been used for many years to prove the existence of an infection. This is particularly necessary when there are not enough microbes to find under a microscope. Some protozoa parasites including trypanosomes, may also be grown outside a living host on artificial media in flasks. There are several types of agar and liquid formulations that can grow human trypomastigotes of *T. cruzi, T. brucei rhodesiense,* and *T. brucei gambiense* and the insect phase—epimastigotes—of *T. cruzi.* If a patient specimen grows either of these parasites, it is proof that the individual has these organisms in his body and is infected.

Inoculation of a rat or a mouse with a patient specimen can be used to show that a trypanosome is present. If the animal gets sick, a specimen from it is examined for presence of the parasite. If rats are used to diagnose *T. brucei rhodesiense,* however, there may be a problem. Sometimes rats naturally carry a trypanosome of their own called *T. lewisi,* acquired from the feces of fleas. The examiner must be aware of this fact and be sure to make the correct identification.

As strange as it may seem, the vector that causes American trypanosomiasis may be used to help make a diagnosis. Disease-free conenose bugs are grown in special laboratories and allowed to bite the patient. If the patient has the disease, the insect should become infected. Examination of the feces of the insect over a period of time determines whether it has the parasite. If the infectious trypanosomes of *T. cruzi* are found, then trypomastigotes were originally present in the patient and the diagnosis is confirmed. This procedure, called **xenodiagnosis**, calls for some degree of caution. Some patients may develop a severe systemic reaction to the bite of conenose bugs.

New molecular methods are revolutionizing the laboratory. The most commonly used is called PCR, or polymerase chain reaction (Figure 7.4). It depends on extracting a pathogen's genetic material from a patient specimen and then making enough copies to work with and test. The specimen DNA is then broken down into manageable pieces by enzymes. They are separated on an agar slab by electrical current. Next molecular probes are applied. They are specific only for the trypanosome DNA the scientist is looking for. If a match occurs, the probes attach and there is a way to detect it. It may be a radioactive tag or a fluorescent color. In the end it is proof of the parasite's existence. This method has been applied to both *T. cruzi* and *T. brucei*.

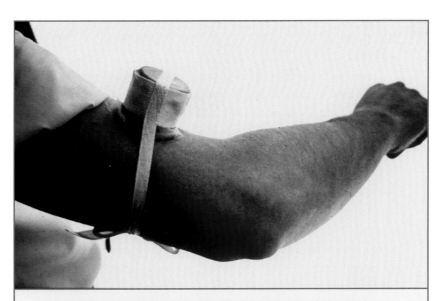

Figure 7.3 Xenodiagnosis allows laboratory-bred, trypanosome-free triatomine bugs to bite a suspected carrier. If present in the patient, *trypanosoma cruzi* will reproduce inside the insect, reaching detectable levels in 30 days. © WHO/TDR

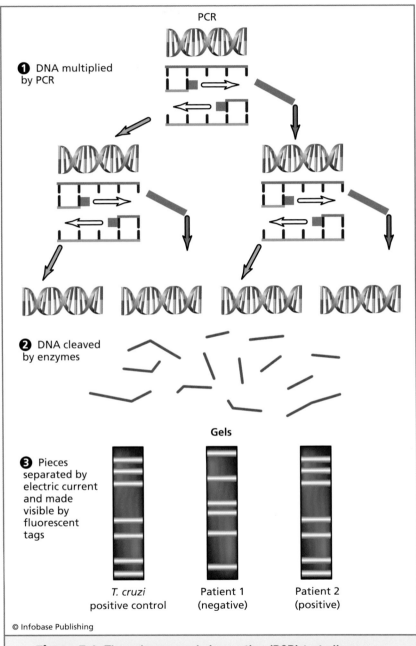

PCR

1 DNA multiplied by PCR

2 DNA cleaved by enzymes

Gels

3 Pieces separated by electric current and made visible by fluorescent tags

T. cruzi positive control

Patient 1 (negative)

Patient 2 (positive)

© Infobase Publishing

Figure 7.4 The polymerase chain reaction (PCR) test allows scientists to reproduce genetic material from pathogens in human specimens. A series of procedures then identifies specific DNA, such as that from a trypanosome.

DETECTION OF *T. CRUZI*

In 2000, the *Journal of Infectious Diseases* reported on the fifth case of American trypanosomiasis acquired in the United States:

"In July 1998, the mother of an 18-month-old boy in rural Tennessee found a triatomine bug in his crib, which she saved because it resembled a bug shown on a television program about insects that prey on mammals. The gut contents of the *Triatoma sanguisuga* were found, by light microscopy and polymerase chain reaction (PCR), to be infected with Trypanosoma cruzi...Whole-blood specimens obtained from the child in July and August were negative by buffy-coat examination and hemoculture but positive by PCR and DNA hybridization, suggesting that he had low-level parasitemia...Two of three raccoons trapped in the vicinity had positive hemocultures for *T. cruzi*. The child's case of *T. cruzi* infection—the fifth reported U.S. autochthonous case—would have been missed without his mother's attentiveness and the availability of sensitive molecular techniques."[26]

The article shows that diagnosis of unusual or rare pathogens is not always easy, and may be missed unless there are clues. Initially the mother of the patient saw a television report and realized that the bug she found might be a vector of disease. She then brought it to the hospital to be tested. Once it was established by two methods (microscopy and PCR) that the triatomine (*T. sanguisuga*) bug carried *T. cruzi*, the next step was to determine whether the patient was infected. Modern DNA testing techniques were used to prove this. In this instance it was determined that raccoons were infected and served as a reservoir in the vicinity. Vigilance, like that of the Tennessee mother, can be key in a correct and speedy diagnosis of unusual infectious diseases.

8

Treatment

Antibiotics are used to treat trypanosomiasis, but there are issues connected to their use that impair their effectiveness. As an example, infections by the staph bacterium, *Staphylococcus aureus*, are widespread. This is a dangerous microorganism and, at one time, penicillin was an effective antibiotic to control it. Throughout the years many types of Staph have changed and become difficult to treat. Methicillin resistant *Staphylococcus aureus* (MRSA) is common and is able to resist therapy by many antibiotics. This dilemma is widespread in the microbial world and pertains to many common pathogens including trypanosomiasis. **Resistance** to antibiotics, unfortunately, is only one of the considerations when providing proper treatment for trypanosomiasis and other infectious diseases.

DRUGS USED TO TREAT TRYPANOSOMES

Treatment for American and African trypanosomiasis may be effective depending on the stage of the disease and the overall health of the patient. Several drugs are used for *T. cruzi, T. brucei rhodesiense,* and *T. brucei gambiense.* This is based on years of experience to find the most useful and least toxic alternatives. Table 8.1 on page 84 summarizes the commonly used treatments.

It is evident from looking at the table that a variety of drugs are used to treat trypanosomes. There is not only a difference between *T. cruz* and *T. brucei,* but even between the two subspecies types of African sleeping sickness, *T. brucei rhodesiense* and *T. brucei gambiense.* In addition, the same disease requires modifications of medication due to age, organs affected, and state of the disease (acute or chronic). Different antibiotics are often needed for brain involvement. Some drugs are very effective for treating trypanosomes in the blood, but not all antibiotics will diffuse across the blood-brain barrier to the spinal fluid. An incorrect selection

Table 8.1 **Common Treatment of Trypanosomiasis**

Type of Disease	Treatment: Blood and Tissue	Treatment: Brain
T. cruzi	Nifurtimox or Benznidazole for acute illness. Treatment not usually helpful for chronic condition.	Same as treatment for acute illness blood and tissue.
T. brucei rhodesiense	Suramin	Melarsoprol
T. brucei gambiense	Suramin or pentamidine isethionate	Melarsoprol (eflornithine if resistant)

will not provide effective concentrations of antibiotic to affect the trypanosomes. In addition, some trypanosomes become resistant to commonly used antibiotics. Specialized drugs are needed in late stage African Sleeping sickness. They are able to go from the circulating blood into the fluid surrounding the brain. Eflornithine is an alternative to the very toxic drug, melarsoprol, but is very expensive to use.

PROBLEMS WITH TREATMENT

Most of us feel confident that if we get sick, a doctor will have an effective drug to treat our illness. Resistance to antibiotics certainly makes this assumption less valid, but there are other concerns as well. One pertains to the type of cells the human body has, compared to those of the infecting organism. The human body has eukaryotic cells, the same type that protozoa have. Medications that destroy the eukaryotic cells of protozoa, such as trypanosomes, are more likely to negatively affect human cells at the same time, since they are so similar. This problem of **toxicity** will produce negative side effects for the patient and make it difficult to select drugs to fight parasites. This is also true for drugs used to treat African and American trypanosomiasis. Melarsoprol, an arsenic based drug used for late-stage sleeping sickness, is so toxic that some patients can actually die from the treatment itself. The patient is hospitalized for close observation during therapy.

Proper drugs will help prevent deaths and improve quality of life. However, there are associated risks that must be taken into account. The goal of treatment is to rid the patient's body of parasites. To do this, the patient must be monitored for signs of effectiveness and for hazardous side effects.

The body's immune system is not always at full strength to aid the effect of therapy. There is a chance that treatment will not work at all. People with acute American trypanosomiasis can be helped when the trypanosomes are in the blood, but treatment is not as effective if the disease is in the chronic stage. It appears that current antibiotics do not have much effect during this phase.

Some new, possibly more effective treatments such as eflornithine for sleeping sickness, are not always utilized in undeveloped countries. American and African trypanosomiasis are typically rural diseases. Medical care is not often available locally and even if it is, newer antibiotics may not be on hand. Hospitals in countries outside of the usual transmission area do not usually stock these rarely used antibiotics. The most widely used drug for advanced African trypanosomiasis, melarsoprol, requires hospitalization for several days or longer. This may not be feasible for the patient or the medical staff. The cost of treatment may also be prohibitive. In the end, circumstances often limit the treatment options for patients with trypanosomiasis. In fact, a number of those infected will never receive medical treatment at all.

OVERALL EFFECTIVENESS OF TREATMENT

There are many complicated factors that determine the outcome of treatment for trypanosomiasis. It is not as simple as taking a pill and feeling better the next day. There are many other concerns that have to do with timely treatment, the most effective antibiotic, cost, resistance of the microbe, and the general health of the patient.

It is best to identify and treat trypanosome infections timely, in the acute stage, when trypomastigotes are in the bloodstream. Drugs are most effective at this time and it is advantageous to stop the progression of the disease before it reaches the brain or develops into a chronic condition. Once symptoms of African trypanosomiasis appear, there will be eventual progression to the brain. Therefore, it is imperative to treat patients close to onset of the illness. In American trypanosomiasis, a chronic condition may last for decades, during which amastigotes reside in the cells and are not adequately affected by treatment. Over the years, major organs are damaged. Often surgery or other supportive care becomes necessary to save the patient.

TRYPANOSOMES FOOL THE IMMUNE SYSTEM

Imagine if you were being attacked by bees and all you had to do was to put on a special ointment to stop the assault. If different types of bees came back the next day, a second kind of ointment would stop them. In fact, to avoid all future encounters with various bees, a limitless supply of assorted ointments would ensure that you would never get stung. This sounds fanciful, but *Trypanosoma brucei rhodesiense* and *Trypanosoma brucei gambiense* are able to do something like this when attacked by the immune system. The outer-protein covering of the trypansomes is vulnerable to antibodies. An individual organism might be killed, but some daughter cells, produced when division takes place, may survive and reproduce. This is because some have different outer-protein coverings than the parent trypanosome.

Trypanosomes that cause sleeping sickness are coated with an antigen called variant surface glycoprotein, or VSG. When the trypanosomes divide, the VSG in a new daughter cell might periodically change its molecular configuration through a process called antigenic variation. This is

Effectiveness of treatment also depends on the virulence of the strain of trypanosome that is affecting the patient. A particular type may cause more extensive damage during a shorter time frame than another. An infection is often more virulent if the patient has an underlying health issue, especially one that weakens the immune system. This can happen with diseases such as AIDS, or as a result of malnutrition. It is well known that age, in general, plays a role in infectious diseases. Children under the age of four or five develop a more acute, life-threatening *T. cruzi* infection than older children. Timely treatment with Nifurtimox or Benznidazole can cure the disease in many cases. A significant number of the older population

medically important for individuals who are infected with this parasite. Antibodies made by affected humans must recognize a particular type of VSG to kill the trypanosomes. If the human immune system detects the antigen of a pathogenic type of *T. brucei rhodesiense* or *T. brucei gambiense* in the bloodstream, it makes antibodies (IgM) against the surface molecule of the trypanosome. However, by the time most of the parasites are killed, a few individuals have different VSG, which current antibodies cannot seek out. These few trypanosomes will multiply to great numbers again. In the meantime the body has to produce new antibodies, and that takes time. The antibodies then attack again, but a few trypanosomes with different VSG survive and multiply. This cycle is repeated over and over again.[27]

This is the reason that African trypanosomiasis is difficult to treat and why patients often suffer recurring bouts of fever, which coincide with the up-and-down population cycle of the parasite. In addition, production of an effective vaccine against ever-changing antigens is very difficult to do.

then suffers from the chronic effects of life long Chagas' disease. In African trypanosomiasis, the younger segment of the population suffers the highest rate of mortality.[28]

FOLLOW-UP TREATMENT

After a patient has American or African trypanosomiasis, he or she has no long-term immunity. A person can survive the disease and still contract it again at a later time. Reinfection can occur if existing circumstances do not change and there is continued contact with the vectors of the disease. Drugs can help reduce the effects of the disease, but the immune system has to help subdue the microbes. In African trypanosomiasis, laboratory examination of spinal fluid for trypanosomes is done for a period of time after a patient has recovered from late stage trypanosomiasis to make sure that the parasites have not reappeared. It is possible that a surviving trypanosome could start multiplying and cause a relapse of the disease, so it is imperative for patients to have follow-up care. On the other hand, patients with chronic American trypanosomiasis have a problem ridding the body of parasites. Without proper antibiotics to treat the long-term infection, the trypanosomes will survive and cause organ deterioration. Supportive surgery and a pacemaker for the heart are needed in many cases to correct the situation.

THE PROBLEM OF RESISTANCE

Everyone has heard a lot of information about antibiotic resistance. Drugs do not always work the way they used to against infectious microbes. This means that several antibiotics that worked previously are no longer effective. How did this happen? If an antibiotic is introduced, it might kill most harmful organisms, but there will be some that are genetically different than most and may be only inhibited by the antibiotic. These will multiply eventually and again reach a very high level. As an example, some bacteria divide every 20 minutes and in eight hours, there will be millions of microbes present. Repeated exposure to the same antibiotic will always select for those genetically fit to survive and they will be the ones left to multiply. These resistant microorganisms may also spread from one person to another and one area to another. Soon these organisms are very widespread. This problem pertains to diseases caused by bacteria, fungi, viruses, and parasites—including trypanosomes.

Some microbes are naturally resistant to specific antibiotics. For others that are initially sensitive to drugs, development of resistance relies on generation time or how fast microbes multiply, their repeated exposures to antibiotics, and evolution.

This is analogous to the struggle between *T. brucei rhodesiense* or *T. brucei gambiense* and the immune system. A genetic change in a few trypanosomes can baffle the immune system for a while and produce another increase in parasite numbers, which worsens the patient illness. Studies in mice have shown that drugs and the immune system work together against trypanosomes. Without a proper immune response, trypanosomes more quickly become resistant to the drug being used.[29]

If an organism must be repeatedly exposed to an antibiotic to become resistant, how does it happen? One way is when patients in hospitals receive antibiotic therapy for a relatively long time as a precaution against infection. If too many antibiotics are used unnecessarily, this can also lead to problems. The more exposure microbes have to antibiotics, the more resistance they may develop. Patients may insist on receiving antibiotics for conditions that will not respond, such as viral infections like the common cold, and doctors may sometimes overprescribe antibiotics in inappropriate situations. The agricultural industry has also been using low-dose antibiotics in animals to stimulate growth and prevent disease. It appears that these antibiotics have caused resistant microbes to develop in the treated animals over a period of time. The concern is that some of these microorganisms may be transferred to humans who are in close contact with the animals. Traces of antibiotics have even been found in

Figure 8.1 Heavy use of antibiotics in domestic animals such as cattle, chicken, or pigs has been reported to contribute to the rise of strains of antibiotic-resistant bacteria. Lynn Betts / Courtesy of USDA Natural Resources Conservation Service

streams and wastewater. Presumably these come from human waste and animal waste, which can contain small amounts of antibiotics, or discarded medicines.

RESISTANCE AND TRYPANOSOMIASIS

The problem of resistance pertains to trypanosomes as well as to bacteria. Protozoa can adapt to a hostile environment in much the same way that bacteria do. Treatment with antibiotics is not always successful and relapses are common. Patients with late-stage African trypanosomiasis are often treated with melarsoprol, for brain involvement. This drug is not always effective in eradicating the trypanosomes.

In animal studies, resistant trypanosomes do not absorb as great a quantity of an antibiotic as more sensitive types do.[30]

They seem to have a way to exclude or pump out the antibiotic and lessen its effects. This is one of the mechanisms that other microbes have evolved also to survive drugs.

To add to the problem, the vectors of American and African trypanosomiasis have, in some cases, developed resistance to the insecticides that are used to control them.

To counteract drug resistance, scientists are working to come up with new and unique ways to fight pathogens. The modern technique of genome analysis has been applied to trypanosomes. Information on gene structure provides researchers a basis for developing drugs and vaccines now and in the future.

Treatment can sometimes save the life of the patient and prevent long-term debilitating disease. However, it is always better to try to prevent an infection from happening initially.

9

Prevention and Health Measures

"An ounce of prevention is worth a pound of cure" is an old saying that has a great deal of truth in it. It basically means that taking a small amount of care at the beginning will prevent big problems in the end. This certainly pertains to avoiding disease. Preventing infection with *T. cruzi, T. brucei rhodesiense* or *T. brucei gambiense* has two benefits. It decreases the chance of dying from an acute infection and helps people avoid severe medical disabilities.

Preventing trypanosomiasis comes down to the difficult task of avoiding bites from insects that transmit the diseases. What can rural people of Africa and South America do on their own and what help can they expect from others? Trypanosomiasis has existed on both continents for centuries and it cannot be controlled by the resident populations alone. Disease control in rural areas on large continents requires a great deal of money and cooperation of many agencies. Both Africa and South America have received some outside assistance to determine the extent of the problem. As an example, the Pan American Health Organization, with local governments in South America, has studied blood bank screening, vector control, education of local residents, and infection status of individuals in different localities. Likewise, in Africa, agencies of the World Health Organization, The United Nations, and others (Africa Union, International Atomic Energy Agency, etc.) have worked on gathering information on African sleeping sickness. Solutions from the data are then provided—medical treatment, preventive measures, and education. The World Health Organization (WHO), through its regional Pan American Health Organization and Pan African Health Organization, the United Nations Children's

Fund (UNICEF), world bank, national governments, private foundations, and pharmaceutical companies are among those that have aligned to implement preventative measures against trypanosomiasis. Canada, Japan, the Bayer Corporation, the Gates Foundation, Doctors Without Borders, and the Carter Foundation are some other organizations that have been active in this effort. The main goal is to break as many links in the chain of disease as possible.

PREVENTION OF AFRICAN TRYPANOSOMIASIS

In Africa, an initial survey of the resident population by medical experts is necessary to find infected humans. These infected people are the primary source of infection in West African trypanosomiasis and just a small part in East African trypanosomiasis. The reservoir, whether human or animal, is a place where tsetse flies can pick up trypanosomes when they bite. Treatment of people and sometimes domestic animals lessens the pool of parasites that may contaminate others. Along with survey and treatment, medical personnel also teach local people how they can reduce the chances of contracting the disease. Studies of the human population, animals, and vectors have been done in the past and are now being done on a continuing basis to keep African trypanosomiasis in check. A breakdown of the system, even for a time, can have important consequences for the populace.

In East Africa, wildlife such as antelope and domestic cattle are the main reservoir for trypanosomiasis. The parasite cycle takes place over a large ecological area and is difficult to control. Unfortunately, some wildlife has had to be killed to try to cut down the number of animal carriers. However, this is not a practical or desirable long-term solution.

As far as the vectors—the tsetse flies—are concerned, fly traps and insecticides are not very effective where the flies do not live in concentrated numbers. An attempt has been made, however, to prevent the breeding of flies by cutting down vegetated breeding areas and applying insecticides by spraying.

This is often not feasible on a vast scale, but is helpful in areas close to where people live.

In West Africa, where flies are more concentrated along rivers, all measures (inspections, spraying and trapping flies, clearing vegetation near villages, treating individuals with infections, and educating the local residents) are employed generally with more success. There can be a more complete reduction of flies in a limited area. It is also helpful that the tsetse flies do not produce a great number of young. They usually mate once for life and produce just one offspring at a time. The total number of young is approximately 10 or less for one female. The lifespan of the fly is about three or four months. Another control measure involves sterilizing or genetically altering male flies and releasing them into the population to compete with normal males. Females that mate with sterile males will not have offspring and the number of flies will decline.[31]

Personal protection, in both areas, lends an added and necessary measure of safety. Bed nets help fend off both mosquitoes that carry malaria and flies that carry trypanosomiasis. It appears that insect repellents applied to the skin cannot be relied upon to offer good protection against tsetse flies. Even with repellant on the skin, the flies will sometimes bite and cause infection. During the day, light-colored clothing that covers most of the body is a good deterrent. The tsetse flies are attracted more to darker colors than light colors.

Prevention of African trypanosomiasis has had success in the past. In the mid-1960s and into the early 1970s, disease transmission was at a very low level, especially in West Africa. At that time, there was good surveillance of the population. Individuals with disease were identified and treated, resulting in fewer infected flies to continue infections. However, intermittent warfare and other factors have had a negative impact on trypanosomiasis prevention by disrupting control measures. In addition, the disease is found over a very large, rural area where funds for prevention are not always

Figure 9.1 Netting around sleeping areas can help ward off biting insects that transmit disease. © subman / iStockphoto

available. An epidemic often generates more interest than low-level endemic diseases, even if more people are involved at the endemic level. It is clear from the past that control

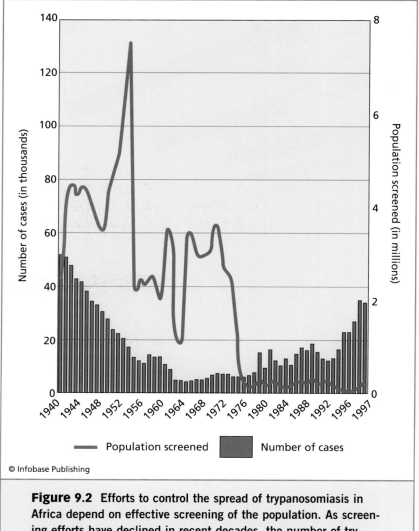

Figure 9.2 Efforts to control the spread of trypanosomiasis in Africa depend on effective screening of the population. As screening efforts have declined in recent decades, the number of trypanosomiasis cases has risen.

of African trypanosomiasis must go on continually so that epidemics are less likely to occur. Epidemics do happen with trypanosomiasis, and they receive proper attention from world health authorities when they do. At present there are many agencies, both public and private, attempting to reduce the number of cases of trypanosomiasis in Africa. The Program Against African Trypanosomiasis (PAAT) is a coordinated effort by four international organizations to help countries affected by African trypanosomiasis. This is essential even in those areas where an epidemic is not taking place at the time.

PREVENTION OF AMERICAN TRYPANOSOMIASIS

Identification of cases of American trypanosomiasis is a useful strategy, just as it is with African trypanosomiasis. Fewer infected individuals in an area reduces the pool of parasites available for the vector to feed upon. This is most important for those with acute disease, who have more trypanosomes in the blood and are more likely to respond to treatment. As in East Africa, the pool of disease is very large and diverse. Perhaps more than 100 different kinds of mammals carry the trypanosomes that cause the disease, so treatment of infected humans is a necessary but small part in overall control. It is impractical and undesirable to try to destroy the reservoir of animals, and so education and strategies of vector control are the main points of attack. The Pan American Health Organization, a regional office of WHO, is working closely with the governments of endemic countries to control American trypanosomiasis.

Since most bites that spread trypanosomiasis occur in the home, the dwelling is a major focus of attention. People are taught how to avoid contact with disease-carrying insects. The educational program has several aspects: Construct or repair homes to eliminate cracks and crevices for conenose bugs to hide, use appropriate insecticides (there is some insecticide resistance), and employ bed nets at night when attacks are probably going to occur. Forest-dwelling conenose bugs are widespread in certain areas and so there have been some more extensive insecticide applications in those places.

There are other ways to acquire American trypanosomiasis besides an insect bite. Transmission by blood transfusion is one method that has resulted in a considerable number of cases. Therefore, screening the blood supply for *T. cruzi* is important to prevent spread of infection.

Testing is done not by checking for the actual microbe, but by searching the donor's blood for antibodies to *T. cruzi*. Finding antibody immunoglobulins indicates that the person has been exposed to *T. cruzi* and may still harbor these trypanosomes. This is the most effective way to screen donated blood, since those with chronic disease have few trypanosomes in the bloodstream. South America has made much progress over the past 10 years in screening for primary pathogens, but there is more to do to ensure a safe blood supply.

The United States tests donated blood for the most common blood-borne pathogens. However, since American

THE BLOOD SUPPLY

In an emergency, a blood transfusion may be lifesaving, but it is imperative that the blood supply is safe and free of pathogens. For this reason, blood banks examine donated blood for organisms known to cause transfusion-related infections, such as HIV, hepatitis B and C, and syphilis. In South and Central American countries, where American trypanosomiasis is prevalent, blood is screened for *T. cruzi*. In the 1990s, governments from the Southern Cone countries (Argentina, Bolivia, Brazil, Chile, Paraguay, and Uruguay), Andean countries (Colombia, Ecuador, Peru, and Venezuela), and Central American countries (Costa Rica, El Salvador, Guatemala, Honduras, Mexico, Nicaragua, and Panama) held meetings to discuss ways to control American trypanosomiasis. They made a commitment to reduce the incidence of disease through all available means, including ensuring the safety of the blood supply. Progress has varied among all these countries and others joining in the effort. However, implementation of strategies has resulted in a positive improvement overall.[32]

trypanosomiasis is rare in the United States, it has not been routinely included in screening tests. Increased immigration and world travel has, however, prompted U.S. blood banks to be more aware of these rare, imported diseases, including American trypanosomiasis. There have been a great number of people from Latin America relocating in the U.S. recently. According to the U.S. Census Bureau, between 2 million and 3 million people from South and Central America immigrated to the United States from 1990 to 1999.[33] Since the chronic form of American trypanosomiasis is present in some of these people, a reservoir now exists. As a result, American blood banks are now considering adding trypanosomiasis to routine screening evaluations. According to a December 2006 release, the FDA has approved a new test and it is expected that American blood banks will soon begin screening for Chagas' Disease.[34] At this point in time, however, potential donors are questioned about world travel, residence in an endemic area, and medical history as part of the screening process. Blood is then refused from those who may have been exposed, either for a specific time period or for life, depending on the circumstances.

VACCINES

At present there are no effective vaccines for *T. cruz, T. brucei rhodesiense,* or *T. brucei gambiense.* The problem with protozoa parasites is that they can easily evade the immune system. The subspecies of *T. brucei* changes its surface regularly to fool the host's immune system. Likewise, genetic variation of *T. cruzi* produces many different strains. A vaccine to stimulate antibodies against one target does not cover all the possible variations. This is similar to facing hundreds of different poisonous snakes and having anti-venom for only one. Despite this problem, researchers are trying to produce protective vaccines for trypanosomiasis.

New genetic technology and international cooperation have allowed the genomes (total genetic material on the chromosomes) of the protozoa responsible for trypanosomiasis to

PRECAUTIONS FOR TRAVELERS

If you ever decide to visit an area where trypanosomiasis is endemic, it is important to be aware of precautions you should take. An excellent place to begin is the Centers for Disease Control and Prevention (CDC). Its Web site contains a special section called *Traveler's Health* that has a lot of good information. You can select your destination or a specific disease to see what you should know about health and safety. In order to travel to certain areas some available vaccinations are required. You should visit your doctor to get the necessary immunizations as a good start to a safe vacation. Unfortunately there are no effective immunizations against *T. cruzi* and *T brucei*, therefore other preventative measures must be taken.

For African trypanosomias, once you reach your destination, you should get local information about the areas of heavy infestation of infective insects so you can avoid them. Wear medium weight, light-colored clothing that covers your entire body. Most insect repellants are not very effective and cannot be relied upon to prevent bites. It is also helpful to use bed netting at night. One interesting behavior of the tsetse fly is its habit of following a dust trail of animals or moving vehicles and looking for a meal. This includes open jeeps, the most common method of conveyance in some parts of Africa. It would be worthwhile to be especially careful of bites during this time.

Avoiding the triatomine bugs in South and Central America is, of course, the best recommendation to defend against American trypanosomiasis. This is most necessary at night when the bugs look for a blood meal. The greatest protection is to spray houses or shelters with insecticide and sleep under a bed net.

Awareness after a vacation is also important. This is probably the time when a previous bite might develop into symptomatic disease. Look for inflamed areas of skin or suspicious symptoms and seek medical help quickly if they appear.

be sequenced. Scientists can now look at the protozoan DNA to plan a prevention strategy. For American trypanosomiasis, a new research approach uses actual pieces of parasite DNA as part of a vaccine under development.[35] This is in contrast to the older, standard method of using a part of the outside wall of the infectious organism as the antigen. Once the DNA enters the host cell, it produces a basic parasite protein, without the infectious parasite. The immune system, recognizing the protein as foreign, makes antibodies to it and, in effect, also to the real parasites if they invade. These proteins are ones that do not change very much from strain to strain and should be effective against many different types. These DNA vaccines have been tested with some success in animals. Unfortunately this vaccine has not been proven in humans and is not available at this time.

Since the *T. brucei rhodesiense* and *T. brucei gambiense* trypomastigote may change its glycoprotein outer layer when it divides inside the human host, another stage in tsetse flies—the epimastigote—is being investigated as the weak link. The epimastigote does not appear to change its outer layer once inside the insect. A vaccine for humans that makes antibodies against these epimastigotes would not initially protect the bitten person against disease. However, the fly would pick up the antibodies against the epimastigotes with the blood meal, and the epimastigotes formed inside the insect would not mature. The transmission would stop for that fly and other flies in a well-vaccinated human population.[36]

A basic approach for both types of trypanosomiasis is to identify specific genes and proteins that cause infectivity in trypanosomes and silence them with drugs or vaccines. With new knowledge and determination, there is hope for the future. There are many ingenious ideas and scientists will not stop until they achieve their goals, no matter how long it takes.

10

World Impact and Future Outlook

In nature, everything is interconnected. Animals, plants, and microbes interact not only with each other, but also with the Earth. Climate has a direct effect on living organisms and the environment in which they live. Many disease-causing microbes are climate-sensitive. A small change, particularly in temperature, can have a great effect on them. In some instances, they may multiply faster or become more aggressive, or the vectors that carry them may become more abundant and widespread. There are often more factors than just temperature involved in the trends of diseases.

The amount of rainfall is also important. Increased rainfall can lead to increased diarrheal diseases caused by the pathogens *Shigella* and *Cryptosporidium*, which can disperse more efficiently in wet weather. Water supplies and agricultural produce may also become contaminated from polluted water at this time. In 1995, *Shigella sonnei*, a bacterium, was implicated in an outbreak in Island Park, Idaho.[37] An abundance of spring rain raised the water table and probably contaminated wells with improperly draining sewage. In another incident a parasite, *Cryptosporidium sp,* sickened thousands of citizens in Milwaukee, Wisconsin.[38] Runoff of fecally contaminated water into Lake Michigan from heavy spring rains probably initiated the problem. Water treatment facilities then were not able to adequately purify the water for consumption. Mice carry the virus that causes hantavirus and deposit the microbe in urine. If rainfall produces more grass seeds than usual, there will be a greater population of mice, and potentially more hantavirus infections in humans.

High humidity, together with warm temperatures, favors growth of molds and pollen-producing plants. These contribute to allergies and asthma in many susceptible individuals. Great increases of plankton due to weather and nutrients (sometimes human pollution) produce blooms of certain species of algae. These secrete toxins that can kill or contaminate aquatic life. Fish and shellfish from these areas may not be suitable for consumption. There is a possibility that people in the area could experience irritation of the mucous membranes and respiratory tract from windblown droplets. In general, even small changes in the climate or environment can have a significant impact on the spread and perhaps pathogenicity of some diseases.

The tropical areas of the world have a burden of infectious diseases, especially diseases caused by parasites. Experts worry that **global warming** will help spread the scope of some tropical diseases. Insects thrive in mild climates, and if there is a warming trend, some will expand their ranges to previously cooler climates. This may be to a higher latitude or to an increased elevation of mountains. If they happen to be vectors that carry infectious organisms, the disease could spread along with the insect populations. Although this likelihood is difficult to prove, there seem to be some examples of this happening. Dengue fever, a mosquito-borne disease, for example, is now more prevalent in Central America, including Mexico, than it has been previously. This increase in distribution may also be happening with ticks that carry diseases. Environmental factors including temperature and rainfall influence the habitats of the tsetse fly and conenose bug. There is a possibility that the range of both types of trypanosomiasis will change also if ecological factors are altered dramatically in the future.

IMPACT OF PARASITES ON THE UNITED STATES

In the United States, one rarely thinks of parasites as a major health problem. We most often hear concerns about diseases caused by bacteria or viruses. It is true that there have been only a handful of American trypanosomiasis cases in the

United States, along with 31 known episodes of imported African trypanosomiasis.[39] There is also a low incidence of malaria in the U.S. and those cases were almost exclusively contracted in foreign countries. In addition, mosquitoes, with their microbes intact, have hitched rides with planes and passengers. This has led to a few instances of "airport malaria" in the vicinity of airports. Worldwide there have been 87 cases from 1969 to 1999.[40]

However, there are some protozoa diseases that are endemic in the United States and that have become epidemic at times. Babesiosis, amebiasis, giardiasis, cyclosporiasis, and cryptsporidiosis are some of these diseases. *Babesia sp* is a protozoan parasite infecting red blood cells and, in this respect, is similar to malaria. Babesiosis is endemic in the United States and transmitted, not by mosquitoes, but by ticks. The other protozoa diseases mentioned primarily affect the intestinal tract and may be contracted from food, water, animals, or another person. The amoeba causing amebiasis can invade other organs, such as the intestine, liver, lungs and brain, if not treated. The Centers for Disease Control and Prevention in Atlanta, Georgia requires that identified infections with many of these be reported. The statistics are tabulated and disseminated to public health agencies and the general public.

THE IMPACT OF TRYPANOSOMIASIS ON THE WORLD

The effects of parasitic diseases are endured by hundreds of millions of people, mainly in the tropical and semitropical parts of the world. Poverty, malnutrition, and lack of access to medical care make the disease load even more difficult for the native population. This is also true for areas where trypanosomiasis is endemic, especially in rural areas. Currently there are factors making trypanosomiasis and other infectious diseases even more widespread than they have been in the past.

One factor is increased migration of people who have infections to other areas of the world. These people constitute a reservoir, and if there are appropriate vectors in the places they go, they may begin a cycle of transmission. Movement, even within the same country, can increase the incidence of disease or spark an epidemic. Some people may be exposed to more insect vectors of the disease or a genetic variation of trypanosome that the body is less able to fight off. This has happened with displaced refugees in Africa. In South and Central America large numbers of people have moved from rural areas to cities. Many of them carry trypanosomes that can cause American trypanosomiasis. This has implications for transmission by conenose bugs and the blood supply.

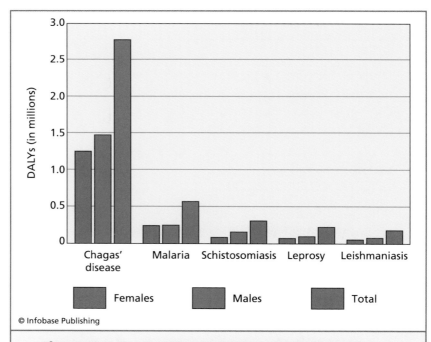

© Infobase Publishing

Figure 10.1 The disability adjusted life years (DALYs) of all patients with Chagas' disease is greater than for many other parasitic diseases in South America. Leprosy, also shown, is a disfiguring disease caused by a bacterium. DALYs represent the total time lost due to disability or premature death.

SOCIAL AND ECONOMIC CONSEQUENCES

There is a great deal of morbidity and mortality with all parasitic diseases, including trypanosomiasis. With millions of cases a year, it is estimated that life expectancy with chronic American trypanosomiasis is decreased by several years. This has an impact on family life and the social structures of communities. African trypanosomiasis has a similar effect on hundreds of thousands of people in Africa.

Economically, these diseases, along with others, make life difficult and tend to create and sustain poverty. Development, which might benefit the local people, is stifled. For example large areas of Africa cannot be opened to human habitation and domestic livestock because of the danger of trypanosomiasis. In addition, trypanosomiasis in animals makes it difficult for the local populace to sustain a living. Domestic cattle are the chief commodity in some areas of Africa. If they cannot survive in a location, the economic fabric of the community is not viable. Often it is not economically feasible to try to control vectors, except in only small areas of the tsetse fly belt. There just are not enough resources to do more.

FUTURE OUTLOOK

In the long term, awareness is the key to controlling trypanosomiasis. There must be continual, uninterrupted observations of the population and vectors. This is the first step that leads to treatment, environmentally sensitive control measures, pertinent education, and improved medical access. It is more effective and lasting to involve local people in all the activities necessary for success. In this way, they take control over their own destinies. Environmental destruction linked to prevention is not a good solution for people in the affected area. To this end, pyrethroid (a substance derived from chrysanthemum plants) insecticides are replacing others that are more persistent and toxic. Other vector control solutions, not relying on insecticides, are being researched.

Disease prevention also requires adequate funding from the more affluent nations. Well-publicized epidemic diseases often take precedence while endemic trypanosomiasis is sometimes temporarily forgotten. There has to be a concerted effort to attack *all* infectious diseases, including those that cause so much misery in the developing world.

Poverty has an indirect effect of sustaining a high infection rate. This may be due to inadequate housing, poor diet, lack of prevention, and minimal access to medical care and educational programs. A real attempt to ease poverty will benefit the future fight against trypanosomiasis and other diseases. One simple goal is the distribution of adequate bed nets throughout Africa and South America, as well as making housing less accessible to insects in South and Central America. Making drugs more available is still a problem that is being addressed in part by WHO along with governments of endemic countries and other organizations. This is a work in progress. Insecticide impregnated bed nets have been distributed, housing is being repaired, vector control programs are in place, and drugs are being distributed. The enormity of the task is daunting in these large undeveloped areas without adequate infrastructures. A continual sustained effort is needed to control and lessen the impact of these forms of trypanosomiasis.

Research is currently being conducted on the many facets of trypanosome diseases. Scientists all over the world are learning about trypanosomes and their vectors to look for effective ways to combat these diseases. The search for more effective drugs and protective vaccines is continuing. In one study, scientists looked to the U.S. Space Agency for help in purifying natural substances as possible drugs. A candidate extracted from a rain forest plant shows potential for blocking key enzymes in the cells of conenose bugs to disrupt disease transmission. Scientists required a suitable quantity of the chemical in pure form for research. In order to speed up the process purified crystals of these enzymes and plant substances have been grown in experiments conducted in

Figure 10.2 A zero-gravity environment allows for the growth of crystals like those seen here, which can help medical researchers find a cure for diseases such as Chagas' disease. © NASA / Photo Researchers, Inc.

space at near zero gravity. Such crystals are larger than those grown on Earth and may help researchers find some solutions for this disease.[41]

Other areas of research and development involve house paint with slow-release insecticide, better field tests for diagnosing American and African trypanosomiasis—such as the CATT test for African trypanosomiasis—and effective non-insecticidal traps for disease carrying insects.[42] Unraveling more information from the genome sequence of parasite and vector will provide necessary information for drugs and vaccines. Better education and communication about disease and prevention is always essential as a primary tool to help prevent contact between individuals and infectious insects.

Trypanosomiasis is an old disease on two continents, but with the benefit of science, it is hoped that the burden from these diseases will be decreased in the near future. The benefit of reducing the rates of trypanosomiasis will not only be for people in the endemic areas, but the entire world.

Glossary

acute—Beginning abruptly, producing intense symptoms, and then subsiding, relatively quickly.

amastigote—A stage in the life cycle of a trypanosomatid protozoa in which the cell does not have any flagella.

anaerobic—Without the presence of oxygen.

antibodies—Protein molecules produced by B cells, in response to infectious agents (antigens) in the body.

antigen—A foreign substance in the body that causes formation of antibodies.

arthropod—A grouping (phylum) of animal life that includes lobsters, crabs, spiders, mites, ticks, and insects.

arthrospores—The asexual reproductive structures of some fungi.

asexual reproduction—A method of forming new organisms without the union of gametes as occurs in budding, fission, and spore formation.

aspirant—Fluid or other material withdrawn from a body cavity or tissue space.

asymptomatic—Showing no symptoms of an infection or other disease

bacteriophage—A virus that infects and may cause destruction of bacteria.

binary fission—The asexual division of a cell into two equal parts, each with complete internal structures.

biomass—The total matter or weight of living organisms.

centrifuge—A laboratory instrument that causes rapid settling of particles in a liquid specimen by spinning and creating centrifugal force.

cercariae—Tiny aquatic forms that enter the human host in the parasitic disease called schistosomiasis.

chagoma—A skin ulcer formed by the bite of a kissing bug carrying *Trypanosoma cruzi*.

chancre—An ulcer of the skin formed by the entry of a pathogen.

chronic—Beginning slowly and lasting for a long period of time.

cilia—The hair-like appendages that propel some protozoa.

colony—A living mass of microbes, usually of one type of organism.

congenital—A condition that is present at birth.

culture—The growth of microbes in the laboratory outside of a host. It is usually done in a petri dish, tube, or flask.

cyst—The resistant capsule form of an organism in the dormant state.

DNA—Deoxyribonucleic acid; a long, coiled molecule that carries and duplicates the genetic information of a living organism.

ecology—The science that deals with the relationships between living organisms and their environment.

ectoparasites—Parasites that live on the skin of human beings or other organisms

endemic—A disease at a low level in a specific geographical area.

epidemic—An outbreak of disease that affects a large number of people at the same time in a geographical area.

epidemiology—The study of the variables that affect the incidence and spread of disease in a certain location.

eukaryote—Organisms (protozoa, algae, animals, and plants) that have cells with a nucleus and organelles surrounded by membranes.

false negatives—Laboratory tests that are negative, but should be positive.

false positives—Laboratory tests that are positive, but should be negative.

flagella—Whip-like appendages that propel some protozoa.

fomite—An inanimate object that contains infectious organisms and can cause an infection.

global warming—The rapid rise of Earth's average temperature due to human activities and pollution.

glycoprotein—A molecule that consists of a protein with a carbohydrate.

homeostasis—The internal equilibrium of the body.

host—An organism that contains and nourishes a parasite.

immunoglobulin—Any of the different types of antibodies formed in the body and present in the serum and other secretions.

intracellular—Inside the cell as opposed to outside the cell.

kinetoplast—A structure where the flagellum originates, in the posterior end of a trypanosome.

lymphatic system—A fluid-carrying network that transports substances throughout tissues of the body.

lymphocytes—White blood cells that produce antibodies and attack antigens.

malaise—A general feeling of illness caused by a disease.

morbidity—The number of illnesses in a population.

mortality—The number of deaths in a population.

motile—Having the power to move spontaneously.

nucleus—A membrane-enclosed structure in eukaryotes that contains the chromosomes and DNA.

opportunistic infections—Infections caused by organisms that are normally not pathogenic, but are able to cause disease particularly in a host with a weakened immune system.

organelle—Specialized structure, found in eukaryotic cells, which is surrounded by a membrane and, performs a specific function for the cell.

Glossary

paleopathologist—A scientist who specializes in studying effects of disease on the bodies of long-deceased humans.

parasite—An infectious organism, usually a pathogenic protozoan or worm, that gains entrance to a host and derives nutrition while harming the host.

pathogenesis—The development or progression of disease in a host.

pathological—Referring to a diseased state.

PCR—Polymerase chain reaction; a molecular laboratory procedure that multiplies DNA copies of infectious microbes found in the body.

periodicity—The state of an event repeating at regular intervals.

prokaryote—Organisms (bacteria) that have cells without a well-defined nucleus or membrane-enclosed organelles.

progressive—Pertaining to the worsening course of a disease over time

pseudopods—The flowing, amoeboid appendages (false-feet) that propel some protozoa.

resistance—The ability of a microbe to defend itself against a specific drug.

schistosomiasis—An infectious disease caused by a parasitic worm of the genus *Schistosoma*.

sporozoa—Immobile parasitic protozoans that have elaborate life cycles, often requiring more than one host.

STD—A sexually transmitted disease.

systemic—Prevalent throughout the organs of the body.

toxicity—The state of being poisonous and producing adverse effects.

transplacental—Passing from the mother through the placenta to the fetus.

trophozoite—The fragile, usually motile form of some protozoa.

trypanosome—A flagellated, pathogenic protozoan of the genus Trypanosoma.

trypomastigote—The flagellated stage of *Trypanosoma cruzi* and *Trypanosoma brucei*.

undulating membrane—The thin, rippling structure along one side of some flagellates.

vector—A living organism that carries and spreads an infectious organism.

virulence—The ability of a microbe to cause disease.

viscera—The internal organs of the body, particularly in the abdominal cavity.

wet preparation—Water is used to hold a living organism for viewing on a microscopic slide.

xenodiagnosis—The use of a laboratory-reared vector to diagnose a patient with an infectious disease.

zoonosis—A disease, originating in animals, that can be transmitted to humans.

Notes

1. Stevens, J. R., and W. Gibson. "The evolution of trypanosomes infecting humans and primates." *Memórias do Instituto Oswaldo Cruz* 93, no. 5 (1998): 669–676.

2. Quotations by Augustus De Morgan. "A Budget of Paradoxes." Available online. URL:, http://www-gap.dcs.st-and.ac.uk/~history/Quotations/De_Morgan.html. Downloaded on May 21, 2006.

3. United Nations Food and Agriculture Organization. Uilenberg, G. *A Fieldguide for the Diagnosis, Treatment, and Prevention of African Animal Trypanosomes.* (adapted from the original edition by W. P. Boyt) Available online. URL: http://www.fao.org/DOCREP/006/X0413E/X0413E00.HTM. Downloaded on March 16, 2006.

4. Kingston, N., E. T. Thorne, G. M. Thomas, L. McHolland, and M. S. Trueblood. "Further studies on trypanosomes in game animals in Wyoming II." *Journal of Wildlife Diseases* 17, no. 4 (1981): 539–546.

5. Herwaldt, B. L., M. J. Grijalva, A. L. Newsome, C. R. McGhee, M. R. Powell, D. G. Nemec, F. J. Steurer, and M. L. Eberhard. "Use of polymerase chain reaction to diagnose the fifth reported US case of autochthonous transmission of *Trypanosoma cruzi*, in Tennessee, 1998." *Journal of Infectious Diseases* 181 (2000): 395–399.

6. Massarani, Luisa. "Fatal Outbreak in Brazil could stem from sugar cane." March 30, 2005. Available online. URL: http://www.scidev.net/News/index.cfm?fuseaction=readNews&itemid=2014&language=1. Downloaded on March 16, 2006.

7. Ibid.

8. Wendel, S., Zigman Brener, M. E. Camargo, and A. Rassi, eds. "Historical Aspects." *Chagas Disease—American Trypanosomiasis: Its Impact on Transfusion and Clinical Medicine.* Sao Paulo, Brazil: ISBT Brazil, 1992. Available online. URL: http://www.dbbm.fiocruz.br/tropical/chagas/chapter.html.

9. Despommier, Dickson D., Robert W. Gwadz, Peter J. Hotez, and Charles A. Knirsch. "American Trypanosomiasis." *Parasitic Diseases*, 5th ed. New York: Apple Tree Productions, L.L.C., 2005. Available online. URL: http://www.medicalecology.org/diseases/d_intro.htm.

10. Herwaldt, B. L., M. J. Grijalva, A. L. Newsome, C. R. McGhee, M. R. Powell, D. G. Nemec, F. J. Steurer, and M. L. Eberhard. "Use of polymerase chain reaction to diagnose the fifth reported US case of autochthonous transmission of *Trypanosoma cruzi*, in Tennessee, 1998." *Journal of Infectious Diseases* 181 (2000): 395–399.

11. "Chagas Disease Following Organ Transplant ." *Morbidity and Mortality Weekly Report.* March 15, 2002. Available online at, http://depts.washington.edu/apecein/newsbriefs/2002/0003nb06.html.

12. America's Blood Centers. "Infections Risks of Blood Transfusion." February 2002, Publication No. 16. Available online at, http://72.14.207.104/search?q=cache:3rcCL1MOz3sJ:www.bloodcenters.org/developments/february2002.pdf+chagas,%22blood+transfusion%22&hl=en&gl=us&ct=clnk&cd=8&ie=UTF-8.

13. Andrew Maykuth online. "New Foe in Battered Africa: Sleeping sickness Report from Sudan. *The Philadelphia Inquirer.* July 18, 1997. Available online at, http://www.maykuth.com.

14. World Health Organization. "African Trypanosomiasis Strategic Direction for Research." Available online at http://www.who.int/tdr/diseases/tryp/direction.htm.

15. University of Chicago. "Virgin Soil Epidemics and Demographic Collapse in Latin America." Available online at, http://72.14.209.104/search?q=cache:Vvd4gYQ0Jy4J:internationalstudies.uchicago.edu/summerinstitutes/epidemics/presentations/jones.ppt+chagas%27,epidemics&hl=en&gl=us&ct=clnk&cd=4&ie=UTF-8.

16. Berrang-Ford, L., O. Berke, L. Abdelrahman, D. Waltner-Toews, and J. McDermott. "Spatial Analysis of Sleeping Sickness, Southeastern Uganda,

1970–2003." *Emerging Infectious, Diseases.* May 2006. Available online. URL: http://www.cdc.gov/ncidod/EID/vol12no05/05-1284.htm. Downloaded June 5, 2006.

17. Cecere, M.C., G.M. Vazquez-Prokopec, R.E. Gürtler, and U. Kitron. "Reinfestation Sources for Chagas Disease Vector, *Triatoma infestans*, Argentina." *Emerging Infectious Diseases*, July 2006. Available online. URL: http://www.cdc.gov/ncidod/EID/vol12no07/05-1445.htm.

18. Sebastia o Aldo Da Silva Balente, Vera da Costa Velente, Habib Fraiha Neto. "Considerations on the Epidemiology and Transmission of Chagas Disease in the Brazilian Amazon." *Memórias do Instituto Oswaldo Cruz*, 94, Suppl I (1999): 395-398.

19. Franks, Jeff.. "Shuttle Commander Sees Wide Environmental Damage" *Reuters*, 4 August 2005. Available online. URL: http://www.commondreams.org/headlines05/0804-02.htm. Downloaded on June 15, 2006.

20. United Nations Food and Agriculture Organization. "Programme Against African Trypanosomiasis." Available online. URL: http://www.fao.org/ag/againfo/programmes/en/paat/home.html. Downloaded on July 15, 2006.

21. Science and Development Network. "Satellite Helps Spot 'Kissing bugs." September 29, 2004. Available online. URL: http://www.scidev.net/content/features/eng/satellite-helps-spot-kissing-bugs.cfm. Downloaded on March 16, 2006.

22. Fackelman, Kathleen. "Patheopathological Puzzles." ScienceNewsOnline. August 23, 1997. Available online. URL: http://www.sciencenews.org/pages/sn_arc97/8_30_97/bob1.htm. Downloaded on March 16, 2006.

23. Moore, David A.J., Mark Edwards, Rod Escombe, Dan Agranoff, J. Wendi Bailey, S Bertel Squire, and Peter L. Chiodini. "African trypanosomiasis in travelers returning to the United Kingdom." *Emerging Infectious Diseases* 8 (2002): 74(3).

24. Bastier, Joseph. "*The Kiss of Death: Chagas' Disease in the Americas—Case studies of Chagas' Disease*," 1998. Available online. URL: http://www.uta.edu/chagas/html/biolHist.html. Downloaded on July 20, 2006.

25. Murray, Patrick R., Ellen Jo Barron, Michael A. Paler, et al., eds. *Manual of Clinical Microbiology*, 7th ed. Washington, D.C.: ASM Press, 1999, pp. 165–166.

26. Herwaldt, B. L., M. J. Grijalva, A. L. Newsome, C. R. McGhee, M. R. Powell, D. G. Nemec, F. J. Steurer, and M. L. Eberhard. "Use of polymerase chain reaction to diagnose the fifth reported US case of autochthonous transmission of *Trypanosoma cruzi*, in Tennessee, 1998." *Journal of Infectious Diseases* 181 (2000): 395–399.

27. Sciencedaily . "Newly Discovered Protein An Important Tool for Sleeping Sickness Research." March 22, 2005. Available online. URL: http://www.sciencedaily.com/releases/2005/03/050308135233.htm. Downloaded on March 16, 2006.

28. Howson, Christopher P., Polly F. Harrison, and Maureen Law, Editors; Committee to Study Female Morbidity and Mortality in Sub-Saharan Africa, Institute Of Medicine. *In Her Lifetime: Female Morbidity and Mortality in Sub-Saharan Africa (1996)*. Available online. URL: http://nap.edu/books/0309054303/html/216.html. Downloaded June 26, 2006.

29. Biotec at Goliat. "New Life for Old Drugs." May 11, 1996. Available online. URL: http://www.bio.net/bionet/mm/parasite/1996-May/001498.html Downloaded on May 28, 2006.

30. Ibid.

31. Despommier, Dickson D., Robert W. Gwadz, Peter J. Hotez, and Charles A. Knirsch. "African Trypanosomiasis" in *Parasitic Diseases*, 5th ed. New York: Apple Tree Productions, 2005. Available online. URL: http://www.medicalecology.org/diseases/d_intro.htm.

32. Moncayo, Alvaro. "Progress towards interruption of transmission of

Chagas' disease." *Mem. Inst. Oswaldo Cruz*, 94, suppl.1 (September 1999): 401–404.

33. U.S. Census Bureau. "Table 5. Legal immigrants by country of birth categories for the federal fiscal year ending September 30, as applied to the vintage 2000 post-censal national estimates: 1990 to 1999." Available online. http://72.14.209.104/u/census? q=cache:1Qc1ULaRaE4J:www.census. gov/population/documentation/ twps0051/tab05.pdf+immigrants&hl=e n&gl=us&ct=clnk&cd=7&ie=UTF-8.

34. USFDA. FDA News. "FDA Approves First Test to Screen Blood Donors for Chagas Disease." December 13, 2006. Available online. URL: http://www.fda. gov/bbs/topics/news/2006/new01524. html. Downloaded December 30, 2006.

35. De Oliveira, Wagner. "New hopes for a vaccine against Chagas disease." July 8, 2004. Available online. URL: http:// www.scidev.net/News/index.cfm?fuseac tion=readNews&itemid=1475&langua ge=1. Downloaded on March 16, 2006.

36. NSERC, Kirsten Rodenhizer. "New Tools to Combat African Sleeping Sickness." March 15, 2000. Available online. URL:, http://www.nserc. ca/science/spark/pearson_e.htm. Downloaded on March 16, 2006.

37. "*Shigella sonnei* Outbreak Associated with Contaminated Drinking Water —Island Park, Idaho, August 1995." *Morbidity and Mortality Weekly Report.*

March 22, 1996. Available online. URL :http://www.cdc.gov/mmwr/ preview/mmwrhtml/00040669.htm. Downloaded May 22, 2006.

38. Commission on Geosciences, Environment and Resources. *Under the Weather: Climate, Ecosystems, and Infectious Disease (2001)*. Available online. URL: http://fermat.nap. edu/books/0309072786/html/56.htm. Downloaded May 29, 2006.

39. Emedicine. "African Trypanosomiasis." Available online. URL: www.emedicine. com/med/topic2140.htm. Downloaded June 1, 2006.

40. World Health Organization. "Airport Malaria: Experts Warn of A Deadly Risk Ready to Land in Many Countries." August 21, 2000. Available online. URL: http://www.who. int/inf-pr-2000/en/pr2000-52.html. Downloaded May 29, 2006.

41. Smith, Michael L. COCORI. "The Kiss of Death." November 1, 1998. Available online. URL: http://www.cocori.com/ library/eco/chagas.htm. Downloaded on March 16, 2006.

42. The UNICEF-UNDP-World Bank-WHO Special Programme for Research and Training in Tropical Diseases. "Chagas' Disease" and "African Trypanosomiasis." Available online. URL: http://www.who.int/ tdr/diseases/chagas/.html and http:// www.who.int/tdr/diseases/tryp/. , Downloaded May 25, 2006.

Books

Bogitsh, Burton J., and Thomas C. Cheng. *Human Parasitology*, 2nd ed. San Diego, CA: Academic Press, 1998.

Brock, Thomas D. *Life at High Temperatures*. Wyoming: Yellowstone Association for Natural Science, History, and Education, Inc., 1994.

Chin, James, ed. *Control of Communicable Diseases Manual,* 17th ed. Washington, D.C.: American Public Health Association, 2000.

Dugard, Martin. *Into Africa*. New York: Doubleday, 2003.

Dyer, Betsey Dexter. *A Fieldguide to Bacteria*. Ithaca, NY: Cornell University Press, 2003.

Garcia, Lynne S., and David A. Bruckner. *Diagnostic Medical Parasitology*, 2nd ed. Washington, D.C.: American Society for Microbiology, 1993.

Murray, Patrick R., Ellen Jo Barron, Michael A. Paler et al., eds. *Manual of Clinical Microbiology,* 7th ed. Washington, D.C.: ASM Press, 1999.

Tierno, Philip M., Jr. *The Secret Life of Germs: Observations and Lessons from a Microbe Hunter*. New York: Simon & Schuster, Inc., 2001.

Varnam, Alan H., and Malcolm G. Evans. *Environmental Microbiology*. Washington, D.C.: ASM Press, 2000.

Wilson, Edward O. *The Future of Life*. New York: Alfred A. Knopf, 2002.

Zimmer, Carl. *Parasite Rex*. New York: Simon & Schuster, Inc., 2001.

Articles

Hagar, J. M., and S. H. Rahimtoola. "Chagas heart disease.", *Current Problems in Cardiology* 20 (1995): 825–924.

Herwaldt, B. L., M. J. Grijalva, A. L. Newsome, C. R. McGhee, M. R. Powell, D. G. Nemec, F. J. Steurer, and M. L. Eberhard. "Use of polymerase chain reaction to diagnose the fifth reported U.S. case of autochthonous transmission of *Trypanosoma cruzi*, in Tennessee, 1998." *Journal of Infectious Diseases* 181 (2000): 395–399.

Herwaldt B.L., and D. D. Juranek. "Laboratory-acquired malaria, leishmaniasis, trypanosomiasis, and toxoplasmosis." *American Journal of Tropical Medicine and Hygiene* 48 (1993): 313–323.

Jelinek, Tomas, Zeno Bisoffi, Lucio Bonazzi, Pieter van Thiel, Ulf Bronner, Albie de Frey, Svein Gunnar Gundersen, Paul McWhinney, and

Bibliography

Diego Ripamonti. "Cluster of African trypanosomiasis in travelers to Tanzanian National Parks (Dispatches)." *Emerging Infectious Diseases* 8 (2002): 634–635.

Kingston, N., E. T. Thorne, G. M. Thomas, L. McHolland, and M. S. Trueblood. "Further studies on trypanosomes in game animals in Wyoming II." *Journal of Wildlife Diseases* 17, no. 4 (1981): 539–546.

Kirchhoff, L. V. "American trypanosomiasis (Chagas' disease)—A Tropical Disease Now in the United States." *New England Journal of Medicine* 329 (1993): 639–644.

————. "American trypanosomiasis (Chagas' disease)." *Gastroenterology Clinics of North America* 25 (1996): 517–532.

Moore, David A. J, Mark Edwards, Rod Escombe, Dan Agranoff, J. Wendi Bailey, S. Bertel Squire, and Peter L. Chiodini. "African trypanosomiasis in travelers returning to the United Kingdom (Dispatches)." *Emerging Infectious Diseases* 8 (2002): 74–76.

Pepin, Jacques, and Bokelo Mpia. "Trypanosomiasis Relapse after Melarsoprol Therapy, Democratic Republic of Congo, 1982–2001." *Emerging Infectious Diseases* 11 (2005): 6.

Sinha A., C. Grace, Alston W. Kemper, F. Westenfeld, and J. H. Maguire. "African trypanosomiasis in two travelers from the United States." *Clinical Infectious Diseases* 29 (1999): 840–844.

Stevens, J. R., and W. Gibson. "The evolution of trypanosomes infecting humans and primates." *Memorias do Instituto Oswaldo Cruz* 93, no. 5(1998): 669–676.

————. "The molecular evolution of Trypanosomatidae." *Advances in Parasitology* 48 (2001): 1–56.

CDs

Morgan, Alan V. "Phanerozoic Eon." *Microsoft Encarta Encyclopedia.* CD ROM. Microsoft, 2002.

Gould, Carol Grant, and James L. Gould. "Animal Distribution." *Microsoft Encarta Encyclopedia.* CD ROM. Microsoft, 2002.

Web sites

A-Z Guide to Parasitology. "Babesia, Trypanosomes, & Leishmania." Available online. at http://www.soton.ac.uk/~ceb/Diagnosis/Vol11.htm.

Alvarez, Lizette. "British Hospitals Struggle to Limit "Superbug" Infections." Available online at URL: http://query.nytimes.com/gst/health/article-page.html?res=9404E7DB153FF937A2575BC0A9629C8B63.

American Association of Blood Banks. "Facts About Blood and Blood Banking."Available online. URL: http://www.aabb.org/All_About_Blood/FAQs/aabb_faqs.htm.

American Society for Microbiology, Academy Colloquia Report. "Health, Climate, and Infectious Disease: A Global Perspective." 1999. Available online. URL: http://www.asm.org/Academy/index.asp?bid=2162.

————. "Preharvest Food Safety and Security" 2004. Available online at http://www.asm.org/Academy/index.asp?bid=33019.

Brower, Jennifer, and Peter Chalk. *The Global Threat of New and Reemerging Infectious Diseases Reconciling U.S. National Security and Public Health Policy.* Available online. URL: http://www.rand.org/publications/MR/MR1602.,

The Carlo Denigri Foundation. Atlas of Medical Parasitology. "Trypanosoma brucei rhodesiense / T.b. gambiense." Available online. URL:, http://www.cdfound.to.it/html/trip2.htm.

————. "Trypanosoma cruzi (Chagas' disease)." Available online. URL: http://www.cdfound.to.it/html/trip1.htm.

Centers for Disease Control and Prevention. "African Trypanosomiasis" Morbidity and Mortality Weekly Report (MMWR) Available online. URL: http://www.cdc.gov/mmwr/preview/mmwrhtml/00001260.htm. Downloaded on March 16, 2006.

————. "American Trypanosomiasis Fact Sheet." Available online. URL: http://www.cdc.gov/ncidod/dpd/parasites/chagasdisease/factsht_chagas_disease.htm. Downloaded on March 16, 2006.

————. "Chagas Disease After Organ Transplantation — United States, 2001.", Available online. URL: http://www.cdc.gov/mmwr/preview/mmwrhtm/mm5110a3.htm. Downloaded on March 16, 2006.

————. "East African Trypanosomiasis Fact Sheet." Available online. URL: http://www.cdc.gov/ncidod/dpd/parasites/trypanosomiasis/factsht_ea_trypanosomiasis.htm. Downloaded on March 16, 2006.

————. "Resurgent Vector-Borne Diseases as a Global Health Problem." Available online. URL: http://www.cdc.gov/ncidod/eid/vol4no3/gubler.htm. Downloaded on March 16, 2006.

Bibliography

————. "Traveler's Health: Yellow Book, Health Information for International Travel, 2005–2006, Chapter 4- Prevention of Specific Infectious Diseases, African Trypanosomiasis." Available online. URL: http://www2. ncid.cdc.gov/travel/yb/utils/ybGet.asp?section=dis&obj=a ftrypano.htm&cssNav=browseoyb. Downloaded on March 16, 2006.

————. "Traveler's Health: Yellow Book, Health Information for International Travel, 2005-2006, Chapter 4- Prevention of Specific Infectious Diseases, American Trypanosomiasis." Available online. URL: http://www2.ncid.cdc.gov/travel/yb/utils/ybGet.asp?section=dis&obj=c hagas.htm&cssNav=browseoyb. Downloaded on March 16, 2006.

————. "West African Trypanosomiasis Fact Sheet." Available online. URL: http://www.cdc.gov/ncidod/dpd/parasites/trypanosomiasis/factsht_wa_ trypanosomiasis.htm. Downloaded on March 16, 2006.

CNN News. "Chagas Disease Found in Ancient Mummies." Available online. URL: http://www.cnn.com/2004/HEALTH/02/03/ancient.disease.ap/. Downloaded on March 16, 2006.

COCORI. "The Kiss of Death.", Available online. URL: http://www.cocori. com/library/eco/chagas.htm. Downloaded on March 16, 2006.

Encyclopedic reference of parasitology. "tsetse flies." Available online. URL: http://parasitology.informatik.uni-wuerzburg.de/login/n/h/1505.html- Downloaded on June 26, 2006.

Environmental Caucus. "Shuttle Commander Sees Wide Environmental Damage" Available online. URL: http://www.environmentalcaucus.org/ global.html. Downloaded on March 16, 2006.

Environmental Health Perspectives. "Infectious Disease: The Human Costs of Our Environmental Errors." Available online. URL: http:// ehp.niehs.nih.gov/members/2004/112-1/focus.html. Downloaded on March 16, 2006.

Geocities. "Vaccine Possibilities for Chagas' Disease" Available online. URL: http://uk.geocities.com/laguz_19/#DTEC. Downloaded on March 16, 2006.

Health Media Lab. "Modern Menace: Emerging and Re-Emerging Infectious Diseases." 2004. Available online. URL: http://www.healthmedialab.com/ html/infectious/modernmenace.html. Downloaded on March 16, 2006.

Institute Of Medicine. "In Her Lifetime: Female Morbidity and Mortality in Sub-Saharan Africa (1996)." Available online. URL: http://darwin.nap. edu/books/0309054303/html/216.html. Downloaded June 26, 2006.

Medical Ecology. "African Trypanosomiasis." Available online. URL: http://www.medicalecology.org/diseases/print_d_african_trypano.htm. Downloaded on March 16, 2006.

———. "American Trypanosomiasis." Available online. URL: http://www.medicalecology.org/diseases/d_american_trypano.htm. Downloaded on March 16, 2006.

Medical Science News. "Scientists Sequence the Genomes of Three Species of Parasites Responsible for Causing Diseases That Kill or Cripple Millions." Available online. URL: http://www.news-medical.net/print_article.asp?id=11740. Downloaded on March 16, 2006.

News-Medical.Net, Disease/Infection News. "Discovery of a Protein JBP2, an Important Tool for African Sleeping Sickness Research." Available online. URL: http://www.news-medical.net/?id=8041. Downloaded on March 16, 2006.

NobelPrize.org. "Alphonse Laveran – Biography." Available online. URL: http://nobelprize.org/medicine/laureates/1907/laveran-bio.html. Downloaded on June 15, 2006.

NSERC, Kirsten Rodenhizer. "New Tools to Combat African Sleeping Sickness." Available online. URL: http://www.nserc.ca/science/spark/pearson_e.htm. Downloaded on March 16, 2006.

Pan American health organization. "Early Warning for Climate Related Diseases." Available online. URL: http://www.paho.org/English/DD/PIN/ptoday16_apr05.htm. Downloaded on June 28, 2006.

———. "IPA* Initiative of the Andean Countries to Control Vectoral and Transfusional Transmission of Chagas Disease." Available online. URL: http://www.paho.org/English/AD/DPC/CD/dch-ipa.htm Downloaded July 14, 2006.

PatientPlus. "African Trypanosomiasis." Available online. URL: http://www.patient.co.uk/showdoc/40000460/. Downloaded on March 16, 2006.

———. "American Trypanosomiasis." Available online. URL: http://www.patient.co.uk/showdoc/40000461/. Downloaded on March 16, 2006.

Rensberger, Boyce. "Special Report: Medical Tales from the Crypt." Available online. URL: http://www.aolsvc.worldbook.aol.com/wb/Media?id=sr193016&st=Medical+Tales+From+The+Crypt. Downloaded on March 16, 2006.

Salyers, Abigail A, Anamika Gupta and Yanping Wang. "Human Intestinal Bacteria as Reservoirs for Antibiotic Resistance Genes." Available online.

Bibliography

URL: http://72.14.209.104/search?q=cache:bsOsPQ6UotwJ:biology.unm.edu/Biol490/NormalFlora.pdf+%22resistance+genes%22,intestine&hl=en&gl=us&ct=clnk&cd=5&ie=UTF-8. Downloaded on June 28, 2006.

Sciencedaily. "Newly Discovered Protein An Important Tool for Sleeping Sickness Research." Available online. URL: http://www.sciencedaily.com/releases/2005/03/050308135233.htm. Downloaded on March 16, 2006.

———. "Researchers Determine How "Hospital Staph" Resists Antibiotics." Available online. URL: http://www.sciencedaily.com/releases/2002/10/021022071006.htm. Downloaded on May 24, 2006.

Science and Development Network. "Fatal Outbreak in Brazil could stem from sugar cane." Available online. URL: http://www.scidev.net/News/index.cfm?fuseaction=readNews&itemid=2014&language=1. Downloaded on March 16, 2006.

———. "New Hopes for a Vaccine Against Chagas Disease." Available online. URL: http://www.scidev.net/News/index.cfm?fuseaction=readNews&itemid=1475&language=1. Downloaded on March 16, 2006.

———. "Satellite Helps Spot 'Kissing bugs.'", Available online. URL: http://www.scidev.net/content/features/eng/satellite-helps-spot-kissing-bugs.cfm. Downloaded on March 16, 2006.

ScienceNewsOnline. "Patheopathological Puzzles." Available online. URL: http://www.sciencenews.org/pages/sn_arc97/8_30_97/bob1.htm. Downloaded on March 16, 2006.

United Nations Food and Agriculture Organization. "African Animal Trypanosomes." Available online. URL: http://www.fao.org/DOCREP/006/X0413E/X0413E02.htm. Downloaded on March 16, 2006.

———. "Programme Against African Trypanosomiasis." Available online. URL: http://www.fao.org/ag/againfo/programmes/en/paat/home.html. Downloaded on July 15, 2006.

Wendel, S , Zigman Brener, M. E. Camargo , and A. Rassi, eds. "Historical Aspects". Available online. URL: http://www.pasteur.fr/recherche/unites/tcruzi/minoprio/tropical/chagas/chapter.html. Downloaded on March 16, 2006.

Whonamedit.com. Biographical Dictionary of Medical Eponyms. Available online. URL: http://www.whonamedit.com Downloaded on June 15, 2006.

Wikipedia Encyclopedia. Available online. URL: http://en.wikipedia.org/wiki/mainpage.

World Health Organization. "African Trypanosomiasis or Sleeping Sickness." Available online. URL: http://www.who.int/mediacentre/factsheets/fs259/en/. Downloaded on March 16, 2006.

———. "African Trypanosomiasis Strategic Direction for Research." Available online. URL: http://www.who.int/tdr/diseases/tryp/direction.htm. Downloaded on June 27, 2006.

———. "Chagas Disease." Available online. URL: http://www.who.int/tdr/diseases/chagas/default.htm. Downloaded on July 15, 2006

———. "Chagas: The Disease." Available online. URL: http://www.who.int/ctd/chagas/disease.htm., Downloaded on March 16, 2006.

———. "Climate Change and Infectious Diseases." Available online. URL: http://www.who.int/entity/globalchange/climate/en/chapter6.pdf. Downloaded on March 16, 2006.

Further Reading and Resources

Books

Ackerman, Jane. *Louis Pasteur and the Founding of Microbiology.* Greensboro, NC: Morgan Reynolds Publishing, 2003.

Buckman, Robert. *Human Wildlife.* Baltimore, MD: The Johns Hopkins University Press, 2003.

Dyer, Betsey Dexter. *A Fieldguide to Bacteria.* Ithaca, NY: Cornell University Press, 2003.

Farrell, Jeanette. *Invisible Allies: Microbes That Shape Our Lives.* New York: Farrar, Straus, and Giroux, 2005.

Fridell, Ron. *DNA Fingerprinting: The Ultimate Identity.* New York: Scholastic Library Publishing, 2001.

Gest, Howard. *Microbes: An Invisible Universe.* Washington, D.C.: ASM Press, 2003.

Koneman, Elmer W. *The Other End of the Microscope.* Washington, D.C.: ASM Press, 2002.

Tierno, Philip M., Jr. *The Secret Life of Germs: Observations and Lessons from a Microbe Hunter.* New York: Simon & Schuster, Inc., 2001.

Varnam, Alan H., and Malcolm G. Evans. *Environmental Microbiology.* Washington, D.C.: ASM Press, 2000.

Viegas, Jennifer. *Parasites.* New York: Rosen Publishing Group, Inc., 2004.

Wilson, Edward O. *The Future of Life.* New York: Alfred A. Knopf, 2002.

Zimmer, Carl. *Parasite Rex.* New York: Simon & Schuster, Inc., 2001.

Web Sites

American Society for Microbiology

http://www.asm.org/

ASM provides microbiology information to professionals and the general public. Microbe World and Microbe Library are two areas, , , , , , to explore.

The Big Picture Book of Viruses

http://www.virology.net/Big_Virology/BVHomePage.html

Those with an interest in viruses will find this site interesting.

The Carlo Denigri Foundation—Atlas of Medical Parasitology

http://www.cdfound.to.it/

An online pictorial atlas of parasitology.

Centers for Disease Control and Prevention/ Division of Parasitic Disease

http://www.dpd.cdc.gov/dpdx/

This is part of the CDC Web site that deals with parasites. It provides a complete overview with text and graphics.

Cells Alive

http://www.cellsalive.com/

Contains information and pictures on microbes as well as other cells.

The Centers for Disease Control and Prevention

http://www.cdc.gov

The premier site to find up-to-date information on pathogens in the United States and abroad.

Cyber Microscope

http://mywebpages.comcast.net/rellstab/ecoscope.htm

Look through the eyepiece into the waters of Antarctica.

Medline Plus

http://medlineplus.gov/

A good source for general medical information.

The Microbe Zoo

http://commtechlab.msu.edu/sites/dlc-me/zoo/zimain.html

Learn about the microbial world around us.

Micrographia,

http://www.micrographia.com/index.htm

Explores the fresh water habitat with microscopy.

The National Institutes of Health

http://www.nih.gov

A good site for all health issues.

National Biological Information Infrastructure

http://www.nbii.gov/education/microbes.html

A link to microbiology education Web sites for grades K–12.

The Pan American Health Organization

http://www.paho.org

This site covers a wide range of topics pertinent to the Americas, including Chagas' disease.

Further Reading and Resources

The World Health Organization

http://www.who.int

This site gives a panoramic view of infectious diseases found all over the world.

Index

AAT (African animal trypanosomiasis), 22–23
acute American trypanosomiasis, 69, 85
acute trypanosomiasis, 33–34, 83
Africa
  displaced refugees, 105
  economic effects of trypanosomiasis, 106
  evolutionary change in *Trypanosoma brucei* structure, 18–19
  exploration of continent by Europeans, 20–21
  origins of continent, 18
  prevention measures in, 92–97
  residence or travel as symptom, 66
  resurgence of trypanosomiasis, 50
  savanna, 9
African animal trypanosomiasis (AAT), 22–23
African trypanosomiasis (African sleeping sickness)
  American trypanosomiasis *vs.*, 40–41
  in animals, 21–23
  case study, 66
  early diagnosis, importance of, 86
  epidemiology, 52–57
  field tests, 109
  follow-up treatment, 88
  geographic distribution, 18–19
  history of, 23–26
  and immune system, 86–87
  laboratory diagnosis, 75
  life cycle, general, 26–28
  life expectancy, 106
  occurrence of, 16, 26, 96
  organs damaged by, 71
  overview, 20–29
  pathogenesis, 65–68

population screening, 96
prevention, 93–97
subspecies of *Trypanosoma brucei,* 28–29
and travelers/tourists, 25, 100
trypanosomiasis protozoan, 17
in U.S., 104
age, and susceptibility to disease, 57, 87–88
AIDS, 7, 71, 87
"airport malaria", 104
algae, 11
allergy, 31, 32, 103
amastigote
  African trypanosomiasis, 40–41
  American trypanosomiasis, 38–41
  in Atacama Desert mummies, 62, 64
  definition, 110
  heart damage by, 73
  and immune system, 45
  in laboratory diagnosis, 75
  leishmaniasis, 49
  of *Trypanosoma cruzi,* 43–44
Amazon rain forest, 57
amebiasis, 104
American trypanosomiasis (Chagas' disease)
  African trypanosomiasis *vs.,* 40–41
  case study, 68–69, 82
  Carlos Chagas' work, 34–35, 37
  coneneose bug as vector, 30–33., *See also* coneneose bug
  diagnosis, 75, 79
  disability adjusted life years, 105
  disease, 33–34
  DNA research, 101
  early diagnosis, impor-

tance of, 86
effect of deforestation, 52
epidemic, 36
epidemiology, 57–59
field tests, 109
follow-up treatment, 88
geographic distribution, 18–19
history, 34
life cycle, general, 38–40
microscopic examination, 77
occurrence, 16, 37–40
overview, 30–41
pathogenesis, 68–69
prevention, 97–99
regions of prevalence, 32
Romaña's sign, 69, 70
screening of blood supply, 97–99
susceptibility of victims, 71
transmission, 32–33
trypanosomiasis protozoan, 17
amoeba, 15–17
anaerobic microbe, 13
Andean countries, 98
animal testing, 79
antelope, 28
antibiotic resistance, 54, 84, 88–91
antibiotics, 54, 68, 83, 85, 88
antibodies, 77, 78, 87, 110
anticoagulant, 29
antigen, 77, 110
archaea, 13
Argentina, 37, 57
Arizona, 32
arthropod, 14, 15, 110
arthrospores, 12, 110
asexual reproduction, 43, 110
aspirant, 75, 110
assassin bug. *See* coneneose bug
asthma, 103
Aswan High Dam, 61

Index

asymptomatic, 110
Atacama desert, 62–64
autopsy, 65
awareness, 106

Babesia, 104
babesiosis, 104
bacteria, 12, 21–22
bacteriophage, 22, 110
barbeiros. See coneneose
bug
bats, 23
B cell, 78
bed nets. *See* netting
Benznidazole, 87
"Bertha" (pseudonymous
Chagas' disease victim),
68–69
binary fission, 43, 110
biomass, 11, 110
bioterrorism, 6
birds, as carriers, 22
blood, 27, 75
blood banks, 99
blood-borne infections, 36
blood fluke, 60
blood meal, 44, 53
blood parasite. *See* trypanosome
bloodstream, 23
blood supply, screening
of, 98
blood transfusion, 34,
36–38, 58, 97–98
Bolivia, 68
brain, 45, 67, 71, 83
Brazil, 34, 36, 37
Bruce, Sir David, 25

California, 38
Canada, 38
cattle, 28, 106
causes, of trypanosomiasis,
17–18
Centers for Disease Control
and Prevention (CDC),
51, 65, 100, 104
Central Africa, 21, 28
Central America, 37, 98, 105

centrifuge, 75, 110
cercariae, 60, 61, 110
Chagas, Carlos, 34–35, 37
Chagas' disease. *See*
American trypanoso-
miasis
chagoma, 8, 110
chancre, 8, 67, 110
children, 71, 87
Chile, 37, 62
chronic, 110
chronic American trypano-
somiasis
effectiveness of medica-
tion, 85
follow-up treatment, 88
immune system defenses,
45
initial infection, 59
life expectancy, 106
organ damage, 71
screening of blood sup-
ply for *Trypanosoma
cruzi*, 98
chronic trypanosomiasis,
32, 34, 37, 83
cilia, 15–16, 110
ciliate, 15–17
climate change, 102
clinical diagnosis, 73
clinical disease, 62–73
Clostridium difficile, 54
Coccidioides immitis, 12
colitis, 54
Collins, Eileen, 59
colon damage, 72
colonization, of Africa, 21
colony, of fungi, 12
colony, 110
coneneose (triatomine)
bug
American trypanosomia-
sis case study, 68, 82
Carlos Chagas' work,
34–35, 37
effect of rainfall on habitat, 103
enzyme research,
107–108

habitat, 32, 61
insecticide control, 57
location of habitat, 61
precautions for travel-
ers, 100
prevention measures, 97
South American distribu-
tion, 33
Trypanosoma cruzi, 39
U.S. trypanosomiasis
cases, 38
as vector, 8, 30–33
xenodiagnosis, 79–80
confusion, as symptom, 66
congenital, 110
congenital infection, 34
contaminated food, 57, 58
continental drift, 18
Cortez, Hernando, 48
Cryptococcus neoformans,
12
Cryptosporidium, 102
CSI (TV show), 64
culture, 79, 110
cutaneous/mucosal leish-
maniasis, 49
cycle, of parasites, 50–51
cyrptosporidiosis, 6
cyst, 44, 47, 110

DALYs (disability adjusted
life years), 105
dark field technique, 47
deer fly, 22–23
deforestation, 52
De Morgan, Augustus, 21
dengue fever, 103
diagnosis, 67, 73–82, 86
disability adjusted life years
(DALYs), 105
distribution, of trypanosomiasis, 18–19
DNA, 13, 80, 81, 101, 110
DNA probe, 67
DNA testing, 65, 82
DNA vaccine, 101
domestic animals, 24,
32–33, 90
drowsiness, 66

Index

Index

About the Author

Donald Kruel has worked with microbes for 25 years. During that time, his primary area of expertise has been microbiology in the medical health field. In this capacity, he has helped identify the causes of a wide range of infectious diseases, including parasites, and has written technical manuals for use in hospital laboratories. He has also worked in the state of Arizona as a public health microbiologist (the parasitology and bacteriology sections) and as an environmental health specialist.

After earning B.S. and M.S. degrees in the biological sciences from the State University of New York, he worked for a time as a conservation biologist and continues to be interested in protection of the environment. In addition, he has taught science at various levels from middle school to community college and is involved with promoting microbiology education. He and his wife Cheryl live in North Carolina.

About the Editor

The late I. Edward Alcamo was a Distinguished Teaching Professor of Microbiology at the State University of New York at Farmingdale. Alcamo studied biology at Iona College in New York and earned his M.S. and Ph.D. degrees in microbiology at St. John's University, also in New York. He had taught at Farmingdale for more than 30 years. In 2000, Alcamo won the Carski Award for Distinguished Teaching in Microbiology, the highest honor for microbiology teachers in the United States. He was a member of the American Society for Microbiology, the National Association of Biology teachers, and the American Medical Writers Association. Alcamo authored numerous books on the subjects of microbiology, AIDS, and DNA technology as well as the award-winning textbook *Fundamentals of Microbiology*, now in its sixth edition.